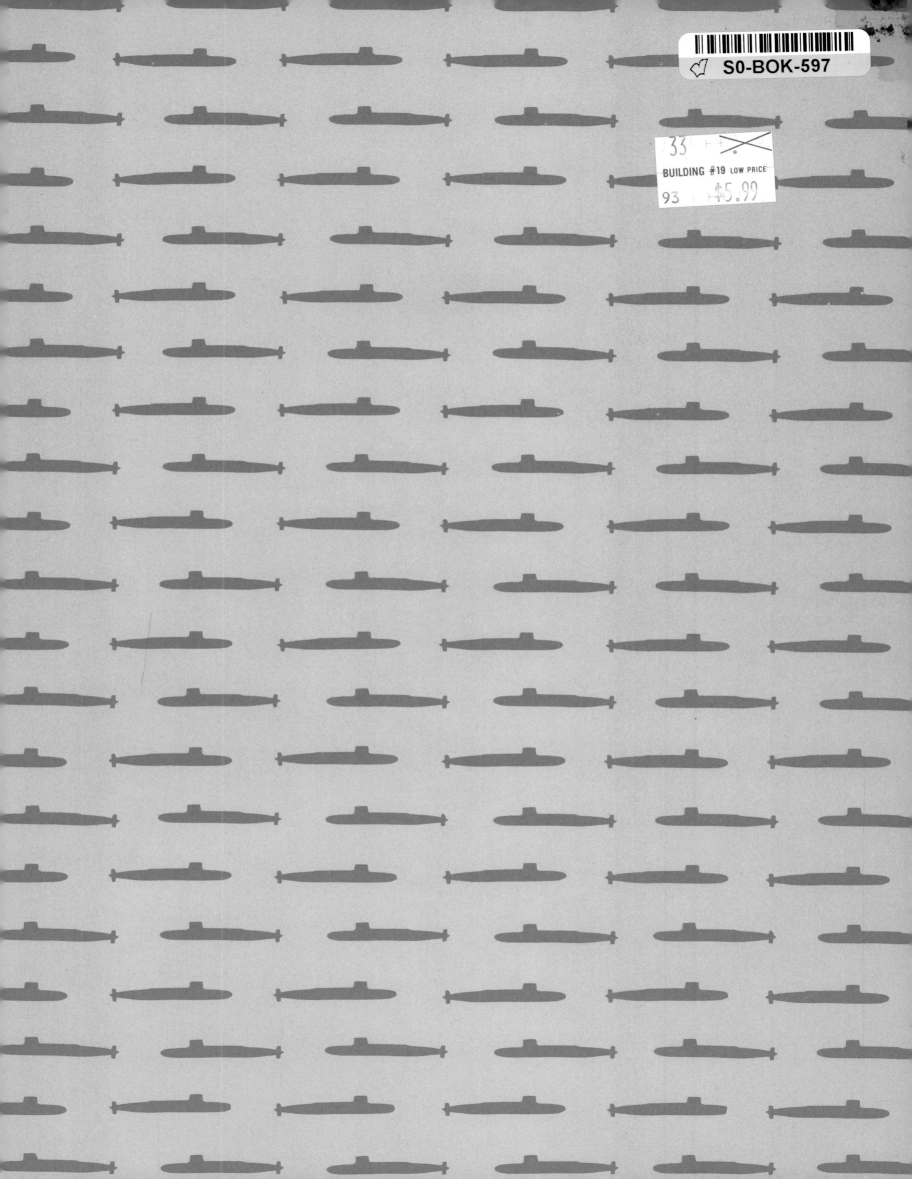

SUBMARINES
HUNTER/KILLERS & BOOMERS

Publications International, Ltd.

Louis Weber, C.E.O.
Publications International, Ltd.
7373 North Cicero Avenue
Lincolnwood, Illinois 60646

Manufactured in Yugoslavia.

h g f e d c b a

ISBN: 0-88176-876-6

Library of Congress Catalog Card Number: 90-60452

Contributing writers:

Andy Lightbody is coauthor of *The Illustrated History of Tanks* and *The Illustrated History of Helicopters*. He is also field/broadcast editor for *Armed Forces Journal International* and is cohost of the weekly military television magazine show "On Target." Mr. Lightbody's articles appear frequently in the national and military trade press.

Joe Poyer, noted military affairs journalist and novelist, is coauthor of *The Illustrated History of Tanks* and *The Illustrated History of Helicopters*. He contributes regularly to numerous military publications, including *International Defense Images* and *International Combat Arms*.

Front cover: The USS Cincinnati *(SSN693), a Los Angeles-class hunter/killer.*

Back Cover: The USS George Washington Carver (SSNBN 656), in Holy Loch, Scotland.

CONTENTS

Pictured: The USS Olympia *(SSN 717) at sunset in Pearl Harbor.*

BEGINNINGS: A TURTLE ATTACKS AN EAGLE

Sergeant Ezra Lee peered through the spray-flecked peephole across the dark waters of New York Harbor. In the gloom of the night, he could just barely make out where his target, the 64-gun British man-of-war HMS *Eagle,* rode at anchor. The surface was choppy and the *Eagle,* dimly lit only by lanterns hung in its rigging and scattered along the docks behind, was difficult to see. It seemed to Lee as if he had been cranking for hours. His arms and shoulders ached badly and his lungs hurt from the lack of fresh air in the stuffy interior. He was also nervously aware of the gunpowder mine that was attached to a long screw extending above his curious craft.

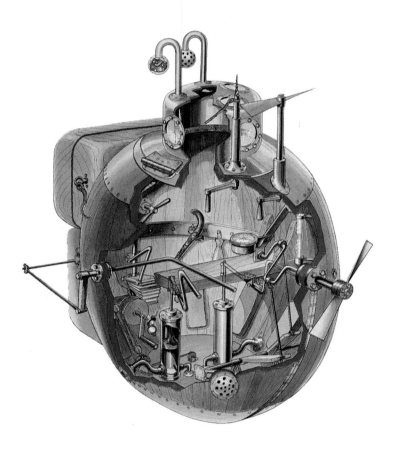

Right: The birth of submarine warfare: A partially submerged Turtle *approaches the HMS* Eagle *in New York Harbor. Above: A detailed look at the* Turtle's *interior, complete with ventilator-pipes protruding from the top, footpedals for cranking the forward-mounted propellor, two ballast pumps beneath the operator's wooden seat, and a bellows-like ventilation pump just behind the operator's seat. Also note the upward-pointing screw for attaching a gunpowder bomb to enemy vessels.*

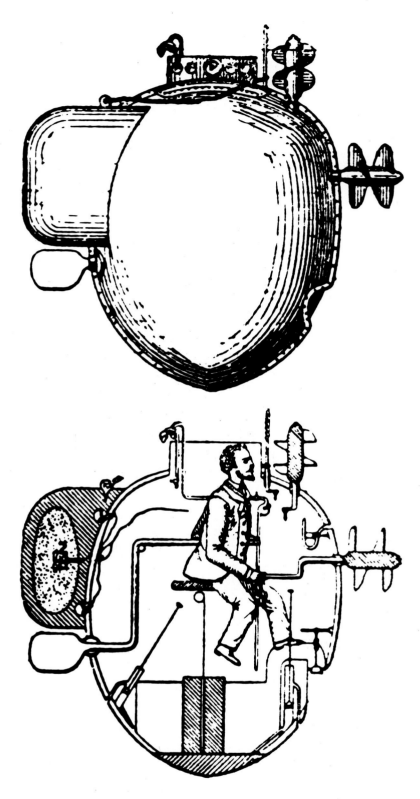

The date was September 6, 1776, and Lee, formerly a foot soldier in George Washington's Continental Army, was now carrying out history's first recorded submarine attack on an enemy warship. He was a volunteer, having accepted this assignment out of patriotism and a sense of commitment to the Revolutionary cause. When he did so, however, it is safe to say that he didn't know what he was getting himself into.

What he had gotten himself into on this night was a small (seven and one-half feet by six feet) acorn-shaped wooden submersible. Its inventor, former Yale student David Bushnell, had named it the *Turtle*. The boat had a brass conning tower with glass peepholes, and was balanced and trimmed with lead ballast. It also had tanks that could be both flooded and emptied with a foot pump. It was powered by a hand-cranked propeller mounted on the front of the craft; a second hand-cranked propeller was mounted on the top for vertical ascents and descents. A conventional rudder, also controlled by hand, was employed to steer the craft.

Although fully submersible, the *Turtle* was severely limited in the length of time it could spend under water. After about thirty minutes, its crew of one would literally have to come up for air. So Lee pressed on, despite the fear and fatigue that now gripped him. The success of his mission did not allow for even the slightest pause in his efforts.

Eventually, Lee did reach HMS *Eagle* undetected. He then submerged and attempted to screw the gunpowder mine into the underside of the ship's hull. Unfortunately, the screw came into contact with an iron strap that connected the *Eagle*'s rudder hinge with the stern. And no matter how hard he tried, Lee could not force the screw into the metal.

Had Lee moved the *Turtle* a few inches to one side or the other, he would have encountered either wood or the copper sheathing commonly worn by ships of that era to protect their hulls from damage by marine organisms. The *Turtle*'s screw was capable of penetrating either material. But Lee could not see what he was doing, and so assumed that the obstruction covered the entire hull. Unable to attach the mine, he withdrew from the scene at dawn. His craft was spotted by a group of British soldiers on Governor's Island, who promptly gave chase in a whaleboat. But when Lee released the mine to float toward his pursuers, the frightened British turned their boat around and rowed back to shore. Lee continued on, finally making it back to his starting point on the southern tip of Manhattan Island some five hours after he had set out.

Above: Two views of the Turtle, drawn in 1885 by F.M. Barber. They were based on a description by the craft's designer, David Bushnell. *Right:* The USS Ohio (SSBN 726), first boat in the class that bears its name. Known as "boomers," ballistic missile submarines like the Ohio are the most powerful weapons systems in the history of warfare.

A few weeks later, the *Turtle* made two more attacks against British shipping. Sergeant Lee piloted the craft on its second mission; an unknown volunteer, on its third. Both attacks were utter failures. The ultimate fate of the *Turtle* is unknown, although it is believed that it was destroyed to keep it out of British hands.

THE MODERN ERA OF SUBMARINE WARFARE

The Paradox of Peace

More than 200 years separate the appearance of the *Turtle* from the commissioning of the USS *West Virginia*, an *Ohio*-class strategic ballistic missile submarine (SSBN) that represents the newest vessel of its kind to enter service in the United States Navy. The difference in offensive capability between the two vessels is truly awesome. In contrast to the *Turtle*'s crude gunpowder bomb, the *West Virginia* carries more firepower in its nuclear arsenal than all the armies and navies of World War I and World War II combined. For that reason this and all ballistic missile submarines are nicknamed "boomers."

The primary adversary of a boomer is the original submarine, the attack submarine (SS). The attack submarine is unofficially referred to as a "hunter/killer."

Two major submarine fleets have developed in the world since 1945. One belongs to the Union of Soviet Socialist Republics; the other, to the United States of America. Other, smaller submarine fleets are also deployed in the world's many oceans, but by and large they are far inferior in firepower and numbers to the underwater fleets of the two superpowers.

Boomers are products of the Cold War, answering a need to establish a balance of power—and terror—to prevent a war far more horrifying than World War II. They represent one leg of a triad of nuclear weapons systems deployed by both the U.S. and the Soviet Union. The other two weapons systems in the triad are airborne nuclear bombs in massive bomber fleets and intercontinental ballistic missiles armed with nuclear warheads.

The chief benefit of these weapons systems is manifested by the condition of relative peace and stability that has

Above: Agent of destruction, guarantor of peace: A submarine-launched Poseidon C-3 missile lifts off from the ocean surface. Below: The USS Salt Lake City (SSN 716), a Los Angeles-class hunter/killer submarine. As the term "hunter/killer" implies, its wartime mission is to seek out and destroy enemy boomers. Opposite Page: Counterpart to America's Ohio boats, this Soviet Yankee I-class boomer carries missiles that are no doubt earmarked for targets on the North American continent.

characterized superpower relations over the past 45 years. This at a time when the United States and the Soviet Union might otherwise have fought a major and devastating war for the control of Europe and Asia, and the political and economic destiny of all humankind. Instead, nuclear weapons have enabled the superpowers to maintain an uneasy, but nonetheless secure truce under a doctrine accepted by both sides and known as MAD—Mutual Assured Destruction.

Of late, superpower relations have been marked by a gradual lessening of mutual hostility. This in turn has lead to substantive efforts by the U.S. and the Soviet Union to negotiate joint reductions in the size of their respective nuclear arsenals. Even the possibility of total nuclear disarmament has been bandied about in some quarters. However, in the unlikely event that nuclear weapons are ever eliminated (and it *is* highly unlikely), nuclear missile-carrying submarines would probably be the last weapons systems to go.

Above: Mortal enemy to Soviet boomers: The USS Cincinnati (SSN 693), a hunter/killer of the Los Angeles *class.* *Below:* Bombers that carry nuclear bombs and/or nuclear-tipped cruise missiles constitute an important leg of the so-called "nuclear triad." *Opposite Above:* U.S. President George Bush and Soviet President Mikhail Gorbachev shake hands at the Malta Summit in December 1989. Although such meetings help to reduce tensions between the superpowers, it is unlikely that they will ever result in the total elimination of ballistic missile submarines. *Opposite Below:* In addition to ballistic missile-carrying submarines, America's nuclear deterrent may be found in silos housing land-based ballistic missiles.

The reason for this is to be found in their extraordinary effectiveness as strategic weapons. Equipped as they are with 20 or 24 nuclear-tipped missiles (each with a range of between 4,000 and 5,000 miles), submarines are nothing more than mobile launching pads that can roam—or hide—virtually at will in the depths of the world's oceans. Not only that, they can maneuver along and under the fringes of the Arctic ice cap, and launch their missiles while remaining safe from detection; they can lie dormant on the ocean bottoms off the coasts of the North American or Eurasian landmasses, waiting for the signal from their national command authorities to launch their deadly cargoes; and they can introduce by the mere fact of their existence a strong element of uncertainty into any military plan that might envision a first strike to destroy the other side's nuclear retaliation capability. That element of uncertainty is enough to make nuclear war seem futile to all but the most foolhardy or irrational leaders.

But suppose a serious political crisis arises in spite of the potential for disaster. In that case, nuclear missile-carrying submarines could be used to threaten the other side with the specter of mass death and destruction. Of course, to be credible such a threat must backed by a willingness to absorb equal levels of punishment in return. What all this amounts to is a giant game of bluff and counter-bluff. Paradoxically, then, peace is maintained by the looming threat of nuclear war—a war that the missile-carrying submarines at once work to prevent and fight with all the horrific means at their disposal.

Above: The Los Angeles-*class hunter/killer USS* Buffalo *(SSN 715) surfaces by using an "emergency blow" of its ballast tanks.* *Below:* A U.S. Lafayette/Franklin-*class boomer with missile tubes open to the air.* *Right:* The waters beneath the northern polar ice cap are a much-frequented haunt of nuclear submarines. The submarine shown here is the USS Whale (SSN 638), a Sturgeon-*class hunter/killer. It shows how Soviet submarines may also punch through the ice to send and receive messages, or launch missiles.*

Boomers and Hunter/killers

As early as 1944, Nazi German naval chiefs began planning a large submarine class to ferry the V-2 ballistic missile across the Atlantic for the purpose of bombarding American and Canadian cities and military targets. In the West, it is widely thought that the Soviets captured many of the German designers who were designing this submarine class. This accounts for the belief that Germans are mainly responsible for post-war Soviet advances in the fields of military science and technology.

Nothing could be further from the truth. In fact, the Western allies captured more German scientists by far than did the Soviet Union. Most of the German scientists captured by the Soviets were merely low-ranking technicians. Thus, the Soviets' military technology advances—in particular, those made in the area of submarine warfare—owe even less to captured German technology and more to their own efforts than do comparable advances made by the Americans.

Of course, it doesn't really matter who was responsible for these advances. The point is, both the American and Soviet navies now have large ballistic missile submarine forces. They operate in much the same pattern. Their task is to patrol as near as possible to the enemy's coastlines without being detected. Since the SSBNs can operate in remote and deep waters, it is extremely difficult to locate them. And, once located, they can quickly and easily disappear.

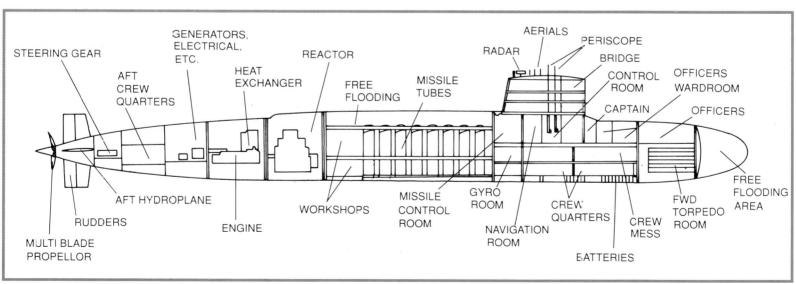

STEERING GEAR
AFT CREW QUARTERS
GENERATORS, ELECTRICAL, ETC.
HEAT EXCHANGER
REACTOR
FREE FLOODING
MISSILE TUBES
RADAR
AERIALS
PERISCOPE
BRIDGE
CONTROL ROOM
OFFICERS WARDROOM
CAPTAIN
OFFICERS
AFT HYDROPLANE
WORKSHOPS
MISSILE CONTROL ROOM
GYRO ROOM
NAVIGATION ROOM
CREW QUARTERS
CREW MESS
FWD TORPEDO ROOM
FREE FLOODING AREA
RUDDERS
ENGINE
BATTERIES
MULTI BLADE PROPELLOR

Above: Looking more like an enormous sea monster risen from the deep than a submarine, a cruising Soviet Typhoon-class boomer churns the sea into a froth. With submerged displacement weights of up to 30,000 tons, the Typhoon boats are the largest undersea vessels ever built. Below: Schematic showing the layout of a typical boomer. Opposite Above: Nazi Germany's V-2 was the world's first ballistic missile, and the prototype for all ballistic missile designs to follow. The Allied victory in Europe in 1945 prevented the V-2's planned deployment on German U-boats, though it was used with considerable success to bombard targets in southern England. Opposite Below: The USS Albany (SSN 753) goes down the ways at its launching ceremony in Newport News, Virginia.

The hunter/killer (attack) submarine follows the original concept of the submarine: to strike from undersea ambush at enemy shipping. The first priority of U.S. hunter/killers is to destroy Soviet boomers. In the event of war, it is imperative that the boomers be eliminated before they can launch their cargo of nuclear-tipped missiles at vital military installations. It is thought that few, if any, submarine launched ballistic missiles on either side are aimed at nonmilitary targets. This is because SLBMs and their associated systems are far too expensive and few in number to waste on targets that can be better handled by land-based missiles.

Above: A hunter/killer of the Victor I *class, thought to be the first Soviet submarine designed specifically for an antisubmarine role. Left: The* Los Angeles-*class hunter/killer USS* Albuquerque *(SSN 706) plows forward through a white-capped sea. The same teardrop-shaped design that makes for smooth travel beneath the waves is often the cause of a rough ride on the surface. Right: The USS* Cincinnati.

Surge

Surge is the term applied to the hypothetical movement made in advance of hostilities by large numbers of boomers and hunter/killer submarines from their bases to their fighting stations.

An explanation as to why an immediate pre-war submarine surge would occur must begin with the understanding that submarines are extremely complex vessels. As such, they are subjected to high levels of physical stress (principally in the form of water pressure) throughout their operational lifetimes. Consequently, their maintenance levels are high. Boats need major overhauls at fairly frequent intervals; new equipment always needs to be installed; crew leave and training take up a great deal of time, as does travel to and from patrol stations. For all these reasons, it is likely that as few as one-third or even 20 percent of the boats in any submarine force are available for combat duty at any given time.

Not infrequently where Soviet submarines are concerned, a 3,600-mile journey, mostly under Arctic ice, must be completed before a boat reaches a typical patrol station in the coastal waters of North America. Assuming a cruising speed of 15 knots, a minimum of 8.5 days would be required to make the trip. (American submarines are faced with the same kind of distances.) Getting their boomers on station and their hunter/killers in a position to protect the boomers is therefore a time-consuming endeavor. To launch a first strike, then, the Soviet national command authorities would have to accelerate maintenance and overhaul schedules, cancel crew leaves, and send their submarine fleet to sea well in advance of the planned start of hostilities.

Of course, this outward surge by Soviet submarine forces would eliminate the element of surprise the Soviet Union would need for a quick and decisive victory. Even in a closed society like the Soviet Union it is not possible to keep secret for long an operation of this magnitude—an operation involving hundreds of thousands of Soviet civilians and naval personnel. Moreover, U.S. surveillance satellites and picket submarines would most certainly detect the movement of large numbers of submarines putting out to sea within days or hours of one another.

Thus the surge would function not only as a prelude to war, but as an early-warning system that might provide the West with precious breathing room in which to formulate a viable response to the Soviet threat.

Like their American counterparts, destroying enemy boomers is a mission that ranks high on the list of priorities for Soviet hunter/killers. But the destruction of enemy surface shipping is also an important concern. The reason for this stems from the Soviets' awareness of NATO defensive doctrine in Europe. This doctrine calls for a holding action along the InterGerman Border (IGB) while massive reinforcements to sustain that effort and convert it to the offensive flow into Europe from the United States and Canada. Since the vast majority of men, materiél, and equipment must be sent by sea, protection of sea lines of communication (SLOC) is vital. The West intends to do so with escorted convoys and patrolling carrier task forces. These convoys and task forces will therefore become a prime target for Soviet hunter/killers.

Above: In contemplating an all-out war between the superpowers, many naval strategists have concluded that aircraft carriers like the USS Kitty Hawk *(CV 63) would be easy pickings for Soviet hunter/killers.* **Right:** *A U.S. carrier battle group in maneuvers. Despite the combined weaponry of many warships and their accompanying aircraft, such battle groups are extremely vulnerable to submarine attack.*

For the most part the Soviet hunter/killers will operate independently of their own aircraft and surface forces. All available evidence indicates that they will achieve a large measure of success in doing so. Recent naval exercises have shown how difficult it is for even the most intensive anti-submarine warfare (ASW) efforts to protect carrier task forces. Given that these exercises were conducted under peacetime safety rules, one can only imagine how much more vulnerable the convoy and carrier task forces will be in time of war. The biggest plume in a Soviet submarine commander's hat would be the destruction of a U.S. nuclear-powered aircraft carrier.

This state of affairs also works to NATO's advantage. The fact that the Soviet Union has fewer surface vessels to protect than their enemies means that NATO hunter/killers can devote more attention to other targets of opportunity. In other words, American, British, West German, Dutch, Spanish, Greek, and Turkish hunter/killer submarines—and possibly even French submarines as well—would be left free to hunt down Soviet boomers and attack boats (submarines are always called boats, not ships).

It should be noted, however, that if the Soviets continue to develop the *Kiev-* and *Kremlin*-class aircraft carriers, American and NATO hunter/killers will certainly have plenty of Soviet surface targets in the event of war.

Above: War between the U.S. and the Soviet Union would probably embroil many other European nations as well. Should that happen, French hunter/killers like the Rubis-*class* Saphir could expect to see plenty of action, presumably against Soviet submarines. *Below:* Though their 16-inch guns still pack a mighty wallop, battleships are no longer the masters of the seas. Replacing them as the capital ships of today's navies are boomer and hunter/killer submarines. *Right:* The Baku, a Soviet Modified Kiev-*class* aircraft carrier, is the kind of target that U.S. hunter/killer crews dream about. Sharing few of the strengths and many of the weaknesses of U.S. aircraft carriers, during a war it would have a hard time protecting itself from submarine attack.

The Oceans

The oceans cover more than 70 percent of the planet, to an average depth of 12,000 feet! This massive body of water is an extremely complex environment fraught with great danger and opportunity alike for the submarines that ply its depths.

Until the third year of World War II, submarines could barely dive their own length. Since then, improved metallurgy, better welding and other joining techniques, more powerful motors to compress air and flush buoyancy tanks, and improved navigational equipment have all combined to increase submarine operating depths. Today, an American *Los Angeles*-class hunter/killer can dive to an estimated depth of 1,400 feet, while boats of the Soviet *Alfa* class can reach depths of nearly 3,000 feet. It is important to grasp that depths of this nature play havoc with the metal hulls of submarines. To avoid premature metal fatigue, all submarines tend to remain at depths between 300 and 600 feet. That means that modern submarines operate in the top ten percent or less of the ocean.

The deepest ocean regions lie far beyond the diving range of modern combat submarines. The surface layers, the coastal waters, and the underwater channels between the landmasses are the areas in which submarines are most active. For the most part, these areas coincide with the

boundaries of the continental shelves. These shelves are really underwater coastal plateaus. They generally slope at an average rate of one degree until they terminate in abrupt drops to the abyssal plains that separate the land-masses. The shelves vary in width from several hundred feet to tens of miles, and their average depth is 400 feet.

Several physical attributes of the oceans directly affect submarine operations. The most important is temperature. A cross section of the ocean can be visualized as being composed of many temperature layers. As one might expect, the relatively warm surface layer is affected by the sun. Curiously, though, solar radiation has less effect on equatorial waters than it does on waters in the higher latitudes. For instance, off the coast of Brazil the sun affects water temperature to depths not exceeding 60 feet. But in the chill waters off the coast of New Brunswick, Canada, solar heating is evident at depths of up to 300 feet.

Below the surface layer, water temperatures decline with depth, but not evenly. The descending temperature layers range from a few inches to several feet thick, and the top layers are usually, but not always, warmer than the layers beneath. A thick layer where temperatures decline rather sharply is called the "permanent thermocline." A thermocline is a layer of water that separates other layers of varying density. The differing density layers are caused by the presence of dissolved and undissolved minerals and salts, soil washed from the land, and plant and animal life. The permanent thermocline is found at depths that vary from 1,000 feet in equatorial waters to as low as 3,000 feet in the higher latitudes.

Beneath the permanent thermocline temperatures fall off at a more gradual rate to the ocean floor. At the bottom, temperatures are cold, but remain fairly constant.

Salinity is another important physical characteristic of the ocean that affects submarine operations. Sodium chloride—salt—is normally dissolved in the oceans at between 32 and 37 parts per thousand. The variation occurs because fresh water run-off, glacial melting, rainfall, and ice formation all act to dilute salt water, which is then unevenly dispersed by currents and convection. Water with a low salt content is lighter. This is the kind of water found in coastal areas, where submarines most frequently conduct operations. In such water a submarine will be less buoyant than it would be in water with a high salt content,

but will submerge at a slower rate because the water in its ballast tanks is relatively light. Conversely, in water with a high salt content, a submarine will be more buoyant, but will submerge faster because the water in its ballast tanks is relatively heavy.

Failure to take into account the effects of differing salinity levels has caused several Soviet submarines to run aground in the low-saline waters off the coast of Sweden.

Submarine commanders must also be aware of the way salinity levels interact with water temperatures. When water layers of differing temperatures meet water layers of differing salinity levels, the result is often severe turbulence. Such turbulence can pose a tremendous danger to modern submarines, which fly through water like aircraft fly through the air. It is possible that turbulence was responsible for the loss of the USS *Thresher,* which sank with all hands off the east coast of the United States in 1963. In all probability, the *Thresher* encountered a pocket of underwater turbulence so violent that it forced the boat down past the hull's ability to withstand water pressure.

This could have happened with shocking rapidity. In the ocean, pressure increases at the rate of 44.45 pounds per square inch per 100 feet. Thus a submarine operating at 1,000 feet experiences 445 pounds of pressure over every square inch of its hull. The *Thresher* was driven down to a depth of 8,500 feet, where the pressure reached 3,782.5 lbs (1.89 tons) *per square inch.* At some terrible point in the *Thresher*'s uncontrolled descent, the ever-increasing pressure on its hull must have crushed the boat with explosive suddenness. For obvious reasons, then, water pressure is another key factor in submarine operations.

Opposite Above: A rare photograph of a submerged U.S. hunter/killer. Opposite Below: Artist's conception of an Ohio-class boomer in its natural element. Right: This illustration of a submarine stalking the ocean's depths imparts an almost science-fiction quality to the undersea realm.

Submarine Propulsion

Submarine nuclear power plants are essentially hot water heaters fueled by Uranium 235. When a neutron strikes the nucleus of a U-235 atom, it knocks, or splits, it. As the nucleus—which is composed of neutrons and protons—splits, energy is released in the form of heat, light, and radioactivity. The newly liberated neutrons then strike and split other U-235 atoms. If sufficient neutrons are available, a self-sustaining chain reaction occurs until the entire mass of U-235 is consumed. Since this chain reaction transpires at near the speed of light, the release of energy is virtually instantaneous and can assume the form of a nuclear explosion.

But if that chain reaction is slowed and controlled, the result is a great deal of heat that can be used to boil water, and certain metals as well. In one type of nuclear reactor, pure water is used as a shielding material, a coolant, and a medium of heat exchange. The liquid is contained in a highly pressurized system of pipes stretching from the reactor to the heat exchanger. In the reactor, the coolant absorbs heat from the fission process and is then pumped to the heat exchanger. There, because it is too radioactive to be used directly, it heats a separate loop of pipes containing uncontaminated water, which subsequently turns to steam.

Most submarines use this steam to drive a turbine connected by gears to the propeller shaft. However, the power plant on one United States submarine, the *Glenard P. Lipscomb,* used the steam to drive a turbo-generator, which produced electricity for the motors that turned the boat's propellers. This turbine electric-drive system did not produce as much power as the direct-steam-drive systems to be found on all other U.S. boats.

The heart of a nuclear power plant is its reactor. Primarily, this consists of a very strong steel casing built to contain the extreme heat developed by the U-235 fuel during the fission process. This process is controlled by metal rods impregnated with neutron-absorbing material (usually cadmium or boron). To slow the chain reaction process, the control rods are inserted into the reactor; to speed up the process, the rods are withdrawn.

If the secondary coolant is a liquid metal like sodium, it too is used to carry the heat away from the heat exchanger to a secondary heat exchanger. There it heats water in a separate system to produce steam that turns a turbine that is connected to the propeller shaft.

There are two ways to control the power output of the nuclear reactor. One involves inserting and withdrawing the aforementioned control rods to speed or slow the fission process and thus increase or decrease the power output. The other method is unique to the pressurized-water reactor, which all U.S. submarines use. It involves withdrawing more steam so as to increase the density of the primary water coolant. As the coolant becomes denser, the neutrons produced by the fission process travel slower. They are thus able to encounter and split more atoms. As more atoms split, more energy becomes available to heat more water. Conversely, easing up on the demand for steam causes the water to become hotter and less dense. Neutrons travel faster and encounter fewer atoms to split, thus causing heat and power levels to fall.

Each system has its advantages and disadvantages. Pressurized-water systems, while more complicated, deal with one less liquid loop. When extremely hot, water for both coolant and the turbo-generator move through the system by natural convection, thereby eliminating the need to run pumps that are inherently noisy (and thus detectable by sonar). But liquid metal-cooled reactors can be made smaller and more powerful. For instance, the lead-bismuth liquid metal-cooled reactors thought to be used in the Soviet *Alfa*-class submarines are half the size of a pressurized-water-cooled system, yet produce between 45,000 and 47,000 hp—a power output capable of driving the boats at submerged speeds of up to 40 knots or more. But this speed is attained at the expense of the noisy pumps that pressurized water-cooled systems don't have.

The only other propulsion system now in widespread use for powering submarines is the diesel engine/electric motor combination. When cruising on the surface, a diesel engine is used to drive the boat and to turn generators that recharge the boat's complement of electricity-supplying batteries. The diesel engine can also use a snorkel to drive the boat at shallow depths. Invented by the Germans during World War II, the snorkel is a long tube that can be raised above the surface to draw fresh air into the boat and to vent exhaust. When the submarine dives below snorkel depth, the diesel engine is shut down and the battery-powered electric motors are switched on.

Right: A nuclear engineering crew member on the USS Daniel Webster *(SSBN 626) enters the boat's reactor compartment. His metallic, heat-reflecting suit is designed to protect him from major steam leaks.*

Being virtually noiseless, an electric motor confers a great advantage to a submarine. But that advantage is more than offset by the rapidity, even at low speeds, with which these boats exhaust their batteries.

The Soviet Union has retained a number of diesel/electric hunter/killer boats in service. They operate primarily in the North Sea and North Atlantic coastal approaches to the Soviet Union. West Germany, France, and Great Britain also operate diesel/electric boats in or near the shallow waters of their respective coasts. The United States has but one conventionally powered submarine in service (USS *Darter*), and it is due to be retired soon.

There is good reason for the near-exclusivity of nuclear-powered boats in the United States Navy. It stems from the fact that the Soviet Union operates the majority of its boomers in Soviet coastal waters or under ice in the Arctic Ocean. To reach these areas, U.S. hunter/killers must travel long distances and remain on station for up to 30 days or more at a time. It is the sort of mission no diesel/electric boat could carry out, at least not without resupply from surface vessels. By the same token, all Soviet boomers are nuclear powered because they must also travel long distances and remain on station for long periods of time.

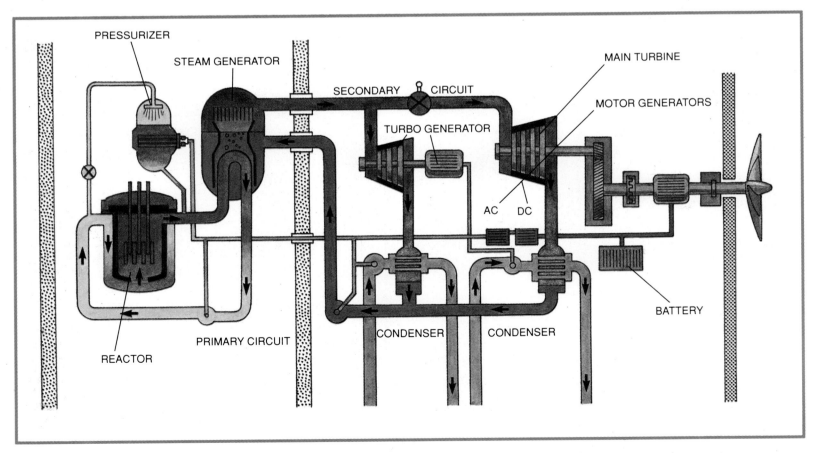

Above: The Soviets retain in service several conventionally powered boats like this Juliett-class cruise missile submarine. They are deployed mainly in the coastal waters of the Soviet Union. Below: As seen here, a nuclear chain reaction can produce an explosion of tremendous force. Yet when properly controlled and channeled, it can also power submarine engines for years at a time. Opposite Below: A schematic showing the basic components of a submarine nuclear propulsion system.

Stealth

These days, the term stealth conjures up visions of strange black aircraft with batlike configurations. But submarines are and always have been the stealthiest of weapons. And the submarine depends on stealth not only for its effectiveness but for its continued existence.

During World War I, the invention of the hydrophone and the first primitive forms of sonar made it imperative that submarines be streamlined and smooth-skinned. Radio wires strung between the conning tower and fantail, and deck guns and other protrusions, had all tended to vibrate at certain speeds and depths.

With the development of nuclear power and the higher underwater speeds that nuclear power made possible, the noise problem could only grow worse. To cope with this problem the United States Navy's first nuclear-powered submarine (*Nautilus,* commissioned in 1955) featured a hull unencumbered by deck guns and a sleek sail with enclosures for the periscope and radar antennae.

Over the years, steady improvements in sonar technology have forced counteracting improvements in submarine stealth technology. One such technology involves the use of hull coatings that absorb sound. Germany pioneered the development of these coatings, and the Soviet Union has refined them to a considerable degree. At present, all Soviet first-line boomers and hunter/killers are coated with anechoic tiles.

These tiles, NATO code-named Cluster Guard, are made of a specially formulated plastics compound to absorb the sound of active sonar. Measuring 12 to 14 inches square and four inches thick, these tiles are affixed with glue to a submarine's metal hull. Intelligence data suggests that they may be pliable enough to "ripple" like the skin of a fish as a submarine moves at high speeds through the water. Such rippling would reduce the friction of the submarine's passage and therefore increase both its speed and range-to-fuel consumption ratio.

Additional information suggests that pipes laid either in or alongside the hull pass a stream of bubbles over the tiles of Soviet submarines. The bubble stream would further reduce friction by making the submarine more "slippery." The bubbles would also add to the anechoic properties of the Cluster Guard tiles.

Submarine Communications

Communicating with or from a submerged submarine is extremely difficult. Since water is opaque to most electromagnetic energy, a submarine is all but cut off from the outside world the moment the waves wash over its conning tower.

How, then, does a submarine transmit information? And how does it receive new orders or intelligence information from the surface?

In answer to the first question, a submarine may eject to the surface a buoy containing sophisticated electronic communications equipment. After a predetermined interval to allow the submarine enough time to leave the area, the buoy will raise an antenna and transmit a taped message to an overhead satellite. To minimize detection, the transmission will be made in a compressed form, or "burst," that lasts only milliseconds. The burst goes out on ultrahigh frequency (UHF) or super high frequency (SHF) bands that travel only in a straight line. Upon completing its transmission, the buoy will then self-destruct.

Aircraft form the basis of an alternative submarine-to-surface communications system. An aircraft drops an electronic buoy that can convert sound waves into UHF transmissions, and vice versa. The submarine sends out its data as sound waves, which the buoy converts into UHF signals and transmits to the aircraft. This system is generally quite effective and the detectability of its transmissions is quite low. However, the presence of a circling aircraft is usually a dead giveaway to the enemy that a submarine is somewhere in the vicinity.

The question of how a submarine receives new orders and information from the surface can be answered by the use of the buoys described above. Another answer can be found in the use of the 124-mile-long buried antenna in Michigan's Upper Peninsula. By broadcasting on extremely low frequencies (ELF) of 0.3 to 3 kilohertz, this communications system can produce transmissions capable of reaching submarines as deep as 300 feet below the surface. ELF messages are extremely slow in transmission and may in fact do nothing more than alert the submarine commander to move nearer the surface to receive a message by other means.

Above: A C-130 TACAMO (Take Charge and Move Out) aircraft takes off on a practice alert from the Naval Air Station in Patuxent, Maryland. Such aircraft are used to communicate with missile submarines hidden deep in the ocean. Because they are mobile, the TACAMO aircraft are less vulnerable to attack than land-based communications centers. *Opposite Above:* Air Force One in flight. From this orbiting command post, the President or his constitutional successor would give the order to launch missiles at the outbreak of war. *Opposite Below:* By 1991, 16 Boeing E-6As like the one shown here are scheduled to replace the C-130s of the TACAMO aircraft fleet. Compared to the C-130, the E-6A has increased speed, longer range, and superior shielding against nuclear blasts. It will serve as the Navy's principal airborne submarine communications link well into the next century.

One of these means involves making very low frequency (VLF) radio transmissions (3 to 30 kilohertz). Under ideal conditions, such transmissions can penetrate at most about 50 feet of water. To receive VLF transmissions, a submarine must either surface or trail a long, buoyant antenna. High frequency radio transmissions are avoided whenever possible. Too many technologically advanced nations deploy equipment that can snatch HF transmissions out of the ether and locate its point of origin in seconds.

Yet another means of communicating with submarines is embodied in the system known as OSCAR (Optical Submarine Communications by Aerospace Relay). OSCAR involves the use of a satellite that matches the speed and rotation of the earth to remain stationary above a fixed spot on the earth's surface. From an altitude of 23,000 miles, this "geostationary" satellite directs a blue-green laser beam at an ocean area where a hunter/killer is on patrol or a boomer is hiding. A message is transmitted by pulsing the laser. The blue-green laser uses the 450-550 nanometer frequencies. The depth at which it can penetrate sea water is classified.

In the event of a nuclear war, a communication from the U.S. National Command Authority (NCA—the president or his constitutional successor) will proceed to its submarines from the National Military Command Authority Center (NMCC) or the Alternate NMCC. The order to launch missiles will proceed from the National Emergency Airborne Command Post to the airborne Boeing E-6A *Hermes* aircraft of the TACAMO (Take Charge and Move Out) system. The E-6As will circle the areas where SSBNs are patrolling and broadcast long-wave radio messages through trailing antennae over six miles long.

The Soviet command authorities use comparable systems to communicate with their submarines. However, the Soviets generally have an easier time of sending and receiving submarine messages. That's because the Soviet Union's main northern submarine bases are situated along the Kola Inlet. From there, Soviet submarines must travel only two to three hundred miles to reach the Arctic ice pack, even in summer. Once beneath the ice, they need only a friendly *polynya* (a Russian word meaning "hole in the ice") to raise a UHF antenna to communicate directly with a satellite. Hidden in the polar ice, a submarine with only its sail or its antennae showing is virtually undetectable by visual surveillance methods. And since broken ice tends to jumble radar signals, it is nearly invisible to radar as well.

Left: The USS Ray *(SSN 653) in the polar ice. After surfacing through the ice, U.S. and Soviet submarines can raise a UHF antenna to establish a communications link with a geostationary satellite.* Above: *A communications buoy in its compartment on the USS* Casimir Pulaski *(SSBN 633). A submerged submarine can eject the buoy to the surface to communicate with an overflying aircraft.* Below: *Long-range communications to submarines are sent from the U.S.Navy Communications Station in Annapolis, Maryland. In view here are towers for transmitting VLF (very low frequency) and ELF (extremely low frequency) messages.*

Submarine Launched Ballistic Missiles

Submarine Launched Ballistic Missiles (SLBMs) are the reason for the boomer's existence. SLBMs are very similar to intercontinental ballistic missiles launched from silos buried deep in the ground. However, these missiles differ from their land-based counterparts in the following respects: they possess more complex navigation equipment (because they do not have a fixed reference point from which to be launched); they are smaller; and their range is shorter.

All U.S. SLBMs are powered by solid-fuel rocket engines, whereas all but two Soviet SLBM types use liquid-fuel propellants. Solid-fuel propellants are more stable and less inflammable than liquid fuels, which can be a decidedly hazardous propellant to use in the close confines of a submarine. At least two Soviet submarines are known to have been lost at sea to fires ignited by the liquid fuel in their missiles. Solid-fuel missiles can also be launched more quickly than liquid-fuel missiles, which must undergo a time-consuming pre-launch procedure involving the pressurization of its fuel tanks and the checking, by computer, of thousands of moving parts. The lesser number of moving parts in solid-fuel missiles also makes them easier to maintain.

Above: A Trident I (C-4), America's premier submarine-launched ballistic missile. It is currently deployed on all SSBNs of the Ohio class, and 12 boats of the Lafayette/Franklin class. Below: The USS Mariano G. Villejo (SSBN 658),a Lafayette/Franklin-class boat modified to take 16 Trident I missiles.

Above: Missile tubes with hatch covers open on a Lafayette/Franklin-class SSBN. *Below:* On October 6, 1986, this Yankee-class Soviet SSBN was fatally damaged 600 miles off the coast of Bermuda when the propellant in one of its missiles exploded. In the aftermath of the explosion, a section of the hull over the boat's third missile tube on the port (left) side can be seen to have been blown completely away. The Soviet vessel sank shortly after this photograph was taken.

The United States has developed three basic SLBMs since the late 1950s: the missiles of the Polaris, Poseidon, and Trident series. Although the Polaris SLBMs have all been withdrawn from U.S. service, the A-3 versions continue to be carried by British Royal Navy SSBNs.

The Poseidon SLBM in current deployment is the C-3. This missile was originally installed on 31 *Franklin* and *Lafayette* boomers. (Twelve of those boats have since been refitted to carry the Trident I.) The C-3 is 34 feet long, 74 inches in diameter, and weighs nearly 65,000 pounds. A two-stage missile with a range of up to 3,200 miles, it carries ten MIRVed warheads, each with a warhead of approximately 50 kilotons yield. (MIRV stands for multiple independent reentry vehicle—a device that carries a single nuclear warhead to a given target.) One variant of this missile carries 14 MIRVs at a reduced range of 2,500 miles. At extreme range, the circular error of probability (CEP) of the C-3 is less than six-tenths of one mile.

The Trident I (C-4) is a three-stage missile with an extreme range of 4,600 miles. It carries eight Mk 4 100-kiloton MIRVs and has a CEP of 500 yards—the length of five football fields. The C-4 is probably the most advanced and deadliest SLBM currently in service. It will be deadlier still when the Mark 500 Evader Maneuvering Reentry Vehicles (MaEV) are installed on all C-4 warheads sometime in the near future. These devices will make it possible for the warheads to effect course-correcting maneuvers during the terminal phase of their reentry. The Trident C-4 is carried by the new *Ohio*-class boomers and 12 *Franklin* and *Lafayette* boats.

The Trident II (D-5), which is scheduled to replace the Trident I on the *Ohio* boats, is a three-stage, solid-fueled missile with a range of 6,000 miles. It will carry either six or seven W87 reentry vehicles, or eight of the older Mk 5 reentry vehicles. The accuracy of the Trident II is said to be equal to that of any land-based missile.

Above: A Poseidon C-3 submarine launched ballistic missile. Though shorter-ranged, less accurate, and less heavily armed with nuclear warheads than the Trident I, it remains in deployment on all but 12 Lafayette/Franklin-class boats. Below: Seen here side-by-side, the Poseidon (left) and the Trident I (right) are the missiles that put the boom in U.S. boomers.

Above: A Trident I displays the kind of rocket's glare that might have inspired the author of the "Star-Spangled Banner." Appropriately, it was launched from the USS Francis Scott Key (SSBN 657), a Trident-missile-carrying boomer of the Lafayette/ Franklin *class.* **Top and Bottom Right:** *Sequential shots of the new Trident II (D-5), launched from the USS* Tennessee (SSBN 734) on August 2, 1989. Scheduled to replace the Trident I on all Ohio-*class boats, the Trident II is superior in range, accuracy, and nuclear warhead payload to all submarine launched ballistic missiles currently in service.*

Opposite Page: Cannisters containing Trident I missiles are loaded aboard the USS Nevada (SSBN 733). The site of this activity is the Explosive Handling Wharf at the Navy's submarine base in Bangor, Washington. Above: A look down a missile tube on the USS Nevada. Below: Workmen ready a missile tube on the USS Nevada for the loading of a Trident I.

Opposite Page: Great care is understandably taken in loading this Trident I into its tube. Should a mishap occur, however, the unarmed nuclear warheads would not explode. **Top Left:** Technicians on the USS Andrew Jackson (SSBN 615, decommissioned in 1988) check missile tubes in the boat's Missile Control Launch Center. **Top Right:** A Trident I missile cannister being readied for loading on board a U.S. boomer. **Below:** The rocket motor of a Trident I missile. It is being X-rayed for flaws at the Strategic Weapons Facility in Bangor, Washington.

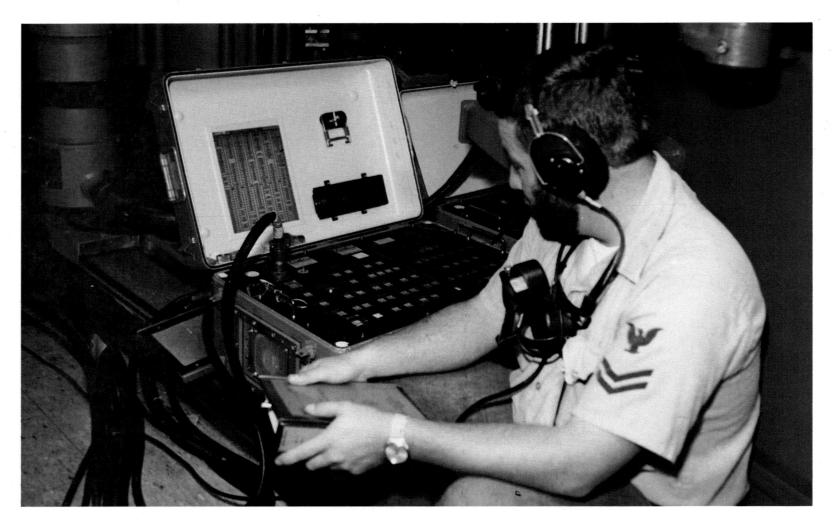

Above: In the Missile Control Launch Center on the USS Ohio (SSBN 726), a technician goes about his business seated with his back against a Trident I tube. *Below:* At the missile launch board in a U.S. boomer. *Opposite:* Missile fire control computers on the USS Daniel Webster (SSBN 626). *Insert:* The "trigger" of a Trident missile-launching mechanism.

Sonar—Eyes and Ears

The heart of a hunter/killer submarine is its electronics. No matter how quiet or how well armed, a hunter/killer is only as good as its detection equipment—and its trained operators. Fortunately for the security of the NATO alliance nations, the U.S. Navy excels in both areas.

Los Angeles-class hunter/killers carry four separate sonar systems to detect enemy submarines and surface vessels. As in most U.S. submarines of its type, one system, the BQQ-5A, is mounted in the bow to sweep the area ahead. Another, the BQR-15, can be released from within the boat's hull and towed behind on a long cable. A third, the BQS-15, works to detect mines the enemy may have planted on the ocean bottom or under the ice where hunter/killer boats do most of their work. The fourth and least-used system is the BQS-13 active sonar.

Passive, or listening, sonar detects sound waves traveling through the water, much like a microphone picks up sounds in the air. The sound wave is converted to electrical energy and measured by delicate instruments to determine the direction (bearing) of the object and its distance (range) from the sending submarine.

Active sonar involves the transmission of a sound wave, which is intercepted when its echo bounces off a solid object. Again, the sound waves are converted to electrical energy to determine bearing and range. Ironically, in finding one's enemy the energy beam put out by active sonar may betray one's presence to the enemy as well. Worse, the enemy may have equipment with which to backtrack the signal to its source. This explains why hunter/killers and navy vessels of all types prefer, whenever possible, the use of passive sonar over active sonar.

A sonar array is simply a series of active and/or passive sonar receivers and transmitters that are grouped and tuned together. By increasing the number of receivers, the sensitivity of the system is increased. Submarines often have sonar arrays mounted on their sides as well as their bows to make them more sensitive. To further enhance the sensitivity of its passive receivers, a submarine may have in tow long strings of sonar receivers that trail well back from the water and noise disturbance (interference) caused by the boat itself.

Once an enemy is detected by the towed array, the submarine might then use its bow-mounted passive sonar system to obtain a second bearing. In this manner, the exact bearing and range of the enemy can be plotted with a great deal of accuracy.

Pictured: Radar control room in a U.S. hunter/killer.

When, despite these efforts, bearing and range cannot be determined with enough exactitude to guide a torpedo to a hunter/killer's prey, the submarine's captain may then resort to active sonar. A very brief burst would be directed at the enemy vessel—too brief, it would be hoped, for the enemy to backtrack. This tactic would be employed only when the submarine captain is fairly certain that the presence of his boat is known to the enemy.

The bottom of the ocean can significantly complicate the use of all types of sonar. This holds true even if the submarine is operating well above the ocean floor. Sonar signals bounce, or are reflected, from solid objects. Submarines depend on this phenomenon to "see" their way in the ocean depths. If the ocean bottom is rocky and irregular, sonar signals will be deflected and return to the source as a confused echo. If the bottom is composed of hills and valleys—as the coastal shelves often are—submarines can hide in sonar shadow much the same way aircraft hide in the radar shadow of high hills and mountains. The navigator must also be aware of the bottom contour if the submarine is to avoid running aground or crashing into an obstruction.

But it is not only solid objects that will reflect sonar signals. The not-quite-solid deep scatter layer (DSL) can reflect and scatter sonar signals as well. The DSL is composed of thick and thin layers of photoplankton and zooplankton. It varies in thickness with the temperature, latitude, and time of day. It also varies in depth. Under normal circumstances it is most dense at midday, when the sunlight causes the microorganisms to multiply and rise toward the surface, and thinnest at night.

In addition to the deep scatter layer, combinations of varying pressure, salinity, and temperature levels can act like solid objects and reflect sonar radiation back toward its transmitting source. Other combinations will create areas that absorb, reduce, or in some way disrupt sonar radiation.

From all this it may be gathered that sonar signals in particular, and sound waves in general are rarely able to travel for long in a straight line underwater. Usually, they also travel faster in areas of greater saline density than they do in areas of lesser saline density. And when entering a layer of greater density, sound waves will bend away from their line of travel; when entering a layer of lesser density, they will be bent back toward their line of travel.

These obstructions to the free transmission of sound all have a tendency to bend sound waves into arcs. Eventually the arcs converge and cancel one another out. The convergence zones where this happens are virtually opaque to sound. Submarine commanders actively seek convergence zones because once in them their boats become invisible to enemy sonar.

Other submarines, and even surface vessels can also take advantage of convergence zones. Sound waves propagate in all directions underwater. When they travel down into deep water they may encounter combinations of pressure, salinity, and temperature that refract them upward. As the sound waves approach the surface, they may encounter similar effects and be reflected downward again. Convergence zones such as these seem to occur at approximately 31-mile intervals. If conditions are right, sound waves can be reflected from convergence zone to convergence zone several times.

Distant sonar receivers can pick up these signals, as can other sonar receivers that have been "dipped" below the convergence zone. For that reason, ASW helicopters will hover, or even land, on the surface and dangle passive sonar receivers deep into the ocean to pick up the sounds of distant submarines.

Above: Inside the sonar dome in the bow of the USS Narwhal *(SSN 671). Bow-mounted sonar is used to sweep the area ahead of a submerged submarine.* ***Right:*** *A sonar operator monitors his console on a U.S. submarine.*

Electronic Warfare

Electronic warfare (EW) can be divided into four parts: ELINT (electronic intelligence); ESM (electronic support measures); ECM (electronic countermeasures); and ECCM (electronic counter-counter measures).

ELINT is intelligence data gathered from any source that emits electronic radiation. These sources might include radio transmitters, radar tracking stations, microwave relay equipment for long-distance telephone calls, and even simple electrical motors.

ESM are those procedures and related equipment used to find and identify electronic radiation. The signal-finding equipment might be sensitive receivers mounted on satellites, aircraft, and ground- and sea-based listening devices. Signals are analyzed by high-speed, high-capacity computers, which compare them to other information gathered in the past. Once identified, a record of the signal is added to various data bases. In the case of submarine-generated signals, these data bases are available to all ASW forces.

Right: An SH-60F Seahawk helicopter lowers a sonobuoy. Once it is "dipped" into the water, the sonobuoy will be used to detect the presence of submerged submarines. Above: A submarine-detecting sonobuoy about to be dipped, as seen from the SH-30 Sea King helicopter that it is attached to.

Above: Both active and passive sonar signals can be used to plot the range and bearing of a submerged submarine. *Opposite:* A crewman loads a sonobuoy onto an SH-60 Seahawk helicopter.

ECM refers to procedures whereby electronic signals are transmitted in such a way as to fool the opposition. The first large-scale use of ECM occurred during World War II, when special Allied units in Scotland and England broadcast bogus radio messages between nonexistent military units. The messages were meant to be intercepted by the Germans, and so they were. From them the Germans learned that the Allies were planning a major invasion of the European continent in either Norway or Greece, or at the Pas de Calais in France. The Nazi intelligence apparatus was not entirely deceived by this stratagem, but they were deceived just enough to have their attention diverted from the real invasion site on the Normandy coastline.

At present, ECM may take several forms. They range from faked radio messages like the kind described above, to sophisticated reproductions of radar signals emitted by a fighter aircraft, to reproductions of engine noises and other ambient sound emanating from a submarine. The object of most ECM techniques is not so much to hide the presence of friendly assets from the opposition as to make them appear to be somewhere other than their actual position.

ECCM can be divided into two phases. In the first phase, measures are taken to remove the veil of misdirection the opposition has thrown around its movements through the use of ECM. Sophisticated computers, complex data analysis and artificial intelligence programs, and skillful and intelligent technicians all play a part in determining whether the signals being received by friendly ELINT receivers are real, or merely decoys.

The protection of one's own equipment and personnel from enemy electronic warfare techniques constitutes the second phase of ECCM. Protection may be achieved by hardening electronic equipment against blast and radiation effects or by using sophisticated jamming techniques to block enemy electronic emissions.

The first step in assessing an enemy threat involves the use of ELINT. For example, consider the measures that might be taken by an American hunter/killer as it searches for a Soviet boomer beneath the Arctic ice sheet. In order to navigate safely through the ice keels hanging down from the Arctic ice sheet, the Soviet boat might be using its ice-detection sonar. This kind of sonar is narrowly focused and usually has a low probability of detection. But if the Soviet boat isn't lucky that day, some trick of differing salinity levels, thermoclines, or current flow might bounce the signal

Decoys

Silencing a submarine to sonar is both expensive and technology-dependent. Within limits, a more cost-effective solution to the problem of remaining hidden lies in the use of decoys.

Both the United States and the Soviet Union have developed highly classified submarine-deployable decoy systems, or "nixies." Whether free-running or towed on a long cable, nixies are designed to simulate the sound of the host submarine so as to decoy the attention of the enemy sonar operators and approaching torpedoes. The free-running nixie is normally a torpedo in which the explosive warhead has been replaced by a small computer and an active sonar transmitter.

If the submarine's sonar detects an approaching torpedo, the boat's captain would react first by diving the boat to gain speed quickly, then by turning away from the torpedo to lengthen his counterreaction time. The captain would then order the release of a nixie. At a set distance from the host, the nixie would begin to transmit recorded sounds and other electromagnetic radiation that would cause the pursuing torpedo to mistake the nixie for the real submarine.

When the new U.S.-developed Mk 48 ADCAP torpedo reaches its terminal phase, a built-in program allows its sonar to distinguish between the target submarine and a nixie. Prior to the terminal phase, signal processors on the torpedo-launching submarine would examine and analyze the relevant signals of the nixie and the target submarine to ascertain their true identity.

toward the American boat. Sonar operators on the American boat would doubtless intercept the signal and recognize it as coming from a Soviet boat.

Following that, the Americans would use ESM to intercept any further signals emanating from the Soviet boat. A BQR-15 towed-array sonar system might be streamed behind the American boat; a WLR-9 sonar receiver might compare any intercepted signals with other signal patterns that were stored in its memory. Thus would the Americans be able to establish the identity, as well as the range and bearing, of the Soviet boat.

Antisubmarine Warfare

A major effort in antisubmarine warfare is devoted to searching for boomers with surface ships, aircraft (both fixed and rotary-winged), and satellites. A variety of techniques for locating submarines are currently employed or under study; they involve quantifying the surface disturbance caused by the wake of a deep-diving submarine and measuring the amount of phosphorescence given off at night by marine organisms disturbed by a submarine's passage.

The most effective antisubmarine weapon is another submarine. The submarines' ability to hide in the vast spaces of the world's oceans have always made them extremely hard to locate and destroy. Before the development of nuclear power, the submarine had to periodically surface, or at least come to within snorkel depth of the surface to operate its diesel engines and recharge its batteries. And even the best diesel/electric boats could not manage much more than 300 miles at 3 to 4 knots submerged or stay submerged more than 12 to 18 hours.

Right: A P-3 Orion overflies a Soviet Victor I *hunter/killer, illustrating the antisubmarine role of such aircraft. P-3s usually carry antisubmarine mines and Mk 46 torpedoes.* **Above:** *The* USS Cincinnati. *A hunter/killer like this* Los Angeles-*class boat is still the best antisubmarine-warfare weapon.*

The nuclear-powered boats, on the other hand, can remain below as long as their provisions hold out. This ability to stay submerged for long periods translates into a corresponding ability to insert themselves into the middle of the most closely guarded task forces.

In 1985, during U.S.-sponsored exercises held off the coast of Japan, three nuclear-powered submarines launched a mock attack on a carrier task force consisting of three large carriers, several cruisers, and numerous destroyers and frigates. The majority of these vessels were employed in an antisubmarine role. Although two of the three nuclear submarines were detected and "sunk," the third hunter/killer sank two aircraft carriers and a cruiser, and then got clean away. In so doing it demonstrated that however effective surface ASW techniques may be, submarines still have the edge in the deadly game of naval warfare.

Right: A depth charge explodes underwater. Within a certain distance, such explosions could produce enough pressure to cave in the hull of a submerged submarine. *Above:* An ASROC (antisubmarine rocket) begins its flight toward an underwater target. A total of 127 U.S. Navy ships are equipped with ASROC systems, which use a short-range ballistic missile to transport either an acoustic torpedo or a nuclear depth charge to the vicinity of an enemy submarine.

Hunter/killer submarines generally operate quite independently of friendly surface vessels and aircraft during ASW operations aimed at enemy boomers and attack boats. Consequently, the hunter/killers are dependent largely on their own resources—which is to say, on sonar and the ability of the crew, particularly the captain, to interpret the data offered by computer analyses of sonar readings.

Yet even though hunter/killers are forced to rely on their own resources when engaged in ASW operations, the smart commander will always make use of surface operations. The activities of friendly ASW surface vessels and aircraft may flush a boomer from its hiding place in the ocean's depths. The boomer thus reveals its presence to the silently stalking hunter/killer, which then moves in for the kill.

Above: The Knox-class *frigate USS* Lockwood *(FF 1064) launches an ASROC.* **Right:** *A carrier battle group, showing the USS* Midway *(CV 41) and the USS* Kitty Hawk *(CV 63). In a naval exercise held in 1985 a battle group like this one "lost" two of three aircraft carriers and a cruiser to a mock attack by three hunter/killers.*

Above: A P-3 Orion on patrol. The P-3 is the U.S. Navy's principal land-based antisubmarine warfare aircraft. Its wartime mission is simply to patrol vast areas of the ocean and bomb anything that constitutes a threat to American territory or ships. *Below and Opposite Above:* Two interior shots of the P-3, showing sonar and radio operators at work. *Opposite Below:* The P-3C Orion, a late-model P-3 variant that carries state-of-the-art computers and electronics for waging antisubmarine warfare. The tail extension on this aircraft carries sensors that can detect the metallic mass of a submerged submarine.

Opposite Page: The submarine is American, which makes its encounter with the SH-60F Seahawk flying overhead a friendly affair. No doubt the atmosphere would be considerably less friendly, if not more exciting for the crews involved, if it were a Soviet boat. *Above:* An SH-60B Seahawk on antisubmarine patrol clatters over its parent ship, the frigate USS Crommelin (FFG 37). Seahawks are generally armed with Mk 46 torpedoes. *Below:* Loading an Mk 46 antisubmarine torpedo on a Seahawk helicopter.

Underwater Weapons

The guided torpedo is the chief underwater weapon of most of the world's navies. Beginning in the 1960s, a variety of missile-launched torpedoes—generically and specifically known as SUBROC, for submarine rocket—were developed and deployed on submarines. SUBROC carries a small nuclear-tipped depth bomb; the missiles that carry the bombs are launched underwater either by letting them float noiselessly from a torpedo tube or by shooting them out with compressed air. The SUBROC floats to the surface and rights itself, whereupon its rocket missile motor ignites and propels it up on a trajectory that takes it to the vicinity of an enemy submarine. The nuclear depth bomb is then released and, when it sinks to a predetermined depth, explodes.

The Soviet SS-N-15 antisubmarine missile is still deployed on non-nuclear hunter/killers of the *Tango* and *Kilo* classes. The United States UUM-44A SUBROC is deployed on eleven *Sturgeon*-class boats, ten *Los Angeles*-class boats, and a few boats of the *Permit* class. Both Soviet and American SUBROCs are now equipped only with nuclear warheads, and both nations are slowly withdrawing them from service because of their limited application. In U.S. service, SUBROC was to have been replaced by the Sea Lance antisubmarine missile in the early 1990s, but the latter system has been cancelled.

The nuclear warhead on torpedoes and antisubmarine missiles are not as powerful as one might think. Nuclear warheads have been developed that are small enough to replace the 600 or so pounds of high explosive in the torpedoes used by submarines of both the Soviet Union and the United States, as well as those of France, England, and China. Yields can range from one-hundredth to about one-tenth of a kiloton equivalent of high explosive. Most submarines—whether made of high-yield steel, stainless steel, or titanium—would be damaged but not destroyed by a 0.01 kiloton-yielding nuclear warhead exploding within about 120 feet. However, if the warhead exploded within 50 feet, it would rupture even the strongest steel double hull. Water increases the destructive power of nuclear explosions close up, but tends to lessen their effect over distance by absorbing their force.

The U.S. Navy currently has the following three torpedoes in service: the Mk 46 lightweight torpedo, which is usually found on aircraft, surface ships, and in the CAPTOR mine; the Mk 37, which is used only in the diesel/electric submarine *Darter;* and the Mk 48 wire-guided heavy torpedo, which is deployed on all other American submarines.

The Mk 48 torpedo is manufactured in three types. The most capable of the three is the new Mk 48 ADCAP

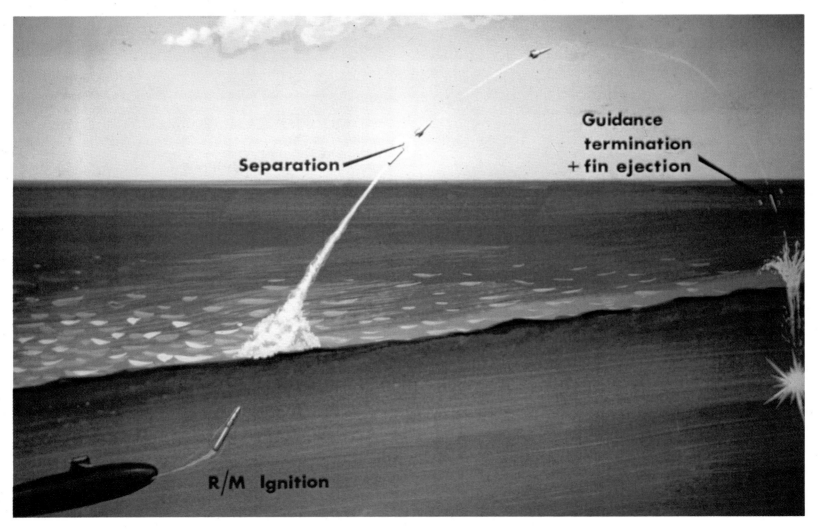

Separation

Guidance termination + fin ejection

R/M Ignition

Opposite: Diagram of a SUBROC antisubmarine missile in action. Top and Left: Crewmen load an Mk 48 torpedo into the USS Haddock (SSN 621). Right: A torpedo retriever boat with an Mk 48 torpedo. The boat has picked up the Mk 48 after a practice run.

(Advanced Capability) torpedo, which was developed to counter advanced Soviet submarines of the *Alfa*, *Sierra*, and *Mike* classes. A new and more powerful active sonar system that can search from side to side over a larger area was built into the Mk 48 ADCAP. The ability of the sonar apparatus to rotate inside its housing relieves the torpedo of having to maneuver while steering toward a target. The Mk 48 ADCAP also travels faster (up to 55 knots) and further than previous Mk 48 types.

The Mk 48 is 21 inches in diameter and 21 feet long. It is powered by a "swashplate" motor—a piston-driven engine that operates like a pump jet and runs on a liquid monopropellant (a propellant that contains both fuel and oxidizer in a single substance).

When launched from a submarine, the Mk 48 remains linked to the host vessel by a thin trailing wire approximately 20 miles long. Guidance commands are sent along the wire from the submarine, which uses its much larger passive sonar to track the enemy. Later versions of the Mk 48 can also use its own sonar to relay acoustic data back to the submarine for processing by the boat's computers.

The instant that the submarine's torpedo operator feels that the sonar aboard Mk 48 has acquired its target, he relinquishes control of the weapon to its own guidance system. The Mk 48 then steers itself the rest of the way to its destination. It will strike an enemy vessel with a warhead that normally contains approximately 650 pounds of a high explosive called PBXN-103.

In contrast to the guided torpedo, mines are a weapon over which the submarine has little control, other than to place them on the ocean floor. Usually mines are installed at so-called "choke points"—areas where landmasses and/or the sea bed interact to form narrow and shallow corridors through which transiting submarines must pass. Mines may contain either nuclear or non-nuclear warheads, and are designed to rest directly on the sea bottom, or float suspended by cables above the bottom. They can remain in place for long periods, although all have a preset self-destruct timer to avoid hazard to shipping after they cease to be of use.

Most mines can be activated by the magnetic field of a passing ship or submarine, or by passive sonar, pressure waves created by passing vessels, or any combination thereof. A less common triggering system is employed by the U.S. Navy's Mk 60 CAPTOR mine. This weapon is essentially a tube containing a Mk 46 homing torpedo. It can be dropped into the ocean by aircraft or ejected through the torpedo tubes of a submarine. The CAPTOR anchors itself to the ocean floor, where it remains until its passive sonar detects a passing submarine. It then launches its torpedo at the hostile boat. Procurement of the CAPTOR has ended far below the Navy's stated goals because of the weapon's cost—$377,000 per unit—and because its warhead, which contains only 96 pounds of explosive, has proven to be disappointingly ineffective.

Above: Crewmen slide an Mk 48 torpedo into the torpedo room of a U.S. hunter/killer. Right: A torpedo is manhandled into its storage berth on board the Quessant, *a conventionally powered hunter/killer of the French* Agosta *class.*

Ocean Floor Detection Systems

The seagoing choke points of the world are heavily monitored by the United States and the Soviet Union, as well as by other nations that belong to neither superpower camp. But only the United States and the Soviet Union can afford to lay and maintain extensive systems of underwater detection sensors outside their national waters.

The United States Navy maintains at least four such systems that it acknowledges publicly. Known as sound surveillance systems (SOSUS), they stretch across the Denmark Strait, the Strait of Gibraltar, off the North Cape of Norway, and across the Bering Strait. It is certain that the U.S. has laid other SOSUS arrays along the coastal shelf approaches to North America and to Western Europe, and in the Davis Strait between Canada and Greenland.

The Soviet Union, in turn, is known to have laid its own version of SOSUS in the Barents Sea, the entrance to the Black Sea, and along the length of the Kurile Islands, which separate the Sea of Okhotsk from the Pacific. The Soviets have probably also laid

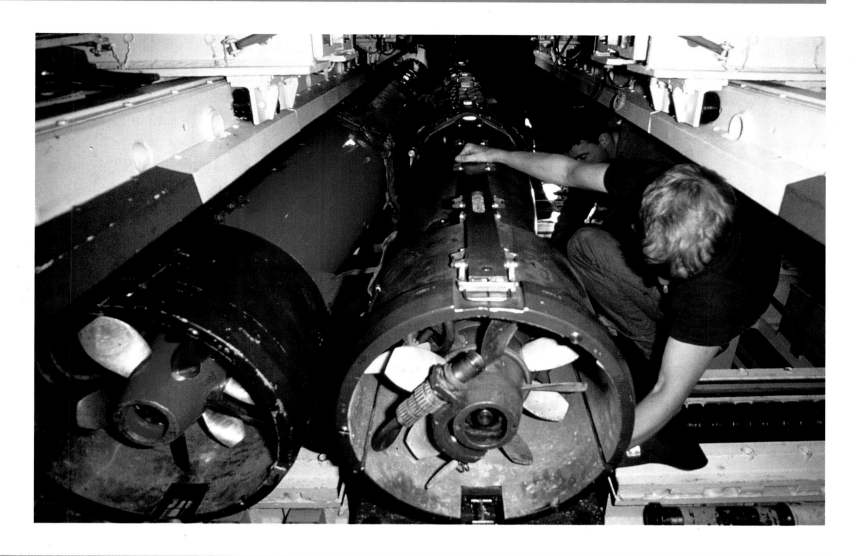

extensive SOSUS arrays in the Sea of Japan and along the Arctic coast approaches to the Soviet Union.

In peacetime, SOSUS arrays keep track of submarine comings and goings. The movements of these boats as well as a record of their sonar signatures are kept in constantly updated intelligence files. During time of war, SOSUS arrays would be used to detect the approach and transit of enemy submarines. This data would then be relayed to American and NATO ASW forces, which would congregate, track, and destroy the intruders.

The first SOSUS arrays were laid on the ocean's floors during World War II. They consisted primarily of hydrophones. By the mid-1950s, these first systems were expanded and replaced by passive sonar arrays that were probably nuclear powered. Currently, Naval Facilities (NAVFACS) s charged with the responsibility for collecting data direct from the SOSUS arrays. From NAVFACS the data proceeds to regional evaluation centers of the Ocean Surveillance Information System (OSIS). From OSIS, the processed information is dispatched to the various United States Navy fleet headquarters in America, Europe, and the Pacific, where it is then distributed to the appropriate naval commands. The data also goes to the Naval Ocean Surveillance Information Center in Maryland, where it is further analyzed before being sent on to the National Command Authorities (NCA) in the White House and the Pentagon.

A number of American and NATO SOSUS arrays have been identified and their locations revealed in Soviet-published journals. It would not be surprising if most or all such arrays have been detected and mapped by both sides. Should war break out, the SOSUS arrays would certainly be early targets for decoy activities, if not outright destruction. But they would serve their purpose by tracking the immediate pre-war movements of enemy submarines, which would have to move out well in advance of the beginning of any hostilities to arrive on station. Detecting such "surges" may well be the most valuable contribution the SOSUS arrays can make to national security.

U.S. AND SOVIET SUBMARINES

U.S. Boomers

Western command of much of the oceans enables American boomers to come relatively close to Soviet territory with little risk of interference by surface antisubmarine warfare (ASW) barriers and hunting parties. That explains why the U.S. Navy needs little more than half the SSBNs than the Soviets to accomplish the same task.

The United States sent its first ballistic missile-carrying submarines to sea in 1959. These *George Washington*-class boats were lengthened versions of the *Skipjack*-class hunter/killer submarines. All five were named after American presidents, and all have been withdrawn from service (the last, the USS *Abraham Lincoln*, was decommissioned in December 1982). They were followed in 1961 by the five boats of the *Ethan Allen* class, which were the U.S. Navy's first purpose-built SSBNs. (The term "purpose-built" means that they were designed from the keel up for a specific purpose, in this case to carry and launch ballistic missiles.) Like the *George Washington* boats, the *Ethan Allen* SSBNs carried the Polaris ballistic missile. The *Ethan Allen* boats are also no longer in service.

Right: The USS Patrick Henry *(SSBN 599), a* George Washington-*class boomer. Boats of this class were the world's first nuclear-powered ballistic missile submarines. When they entered service in the early 1960s, they introduced a radical new element into the competition for strategic advantage between the U.S. and Soviet Union.* **Above:** *The USS* John Marshall *(SSN 611), an* Ethan Allen-*class boomer. The boats of this class were converted into hunter/killers before they were decommissioned in the late 1980s.*

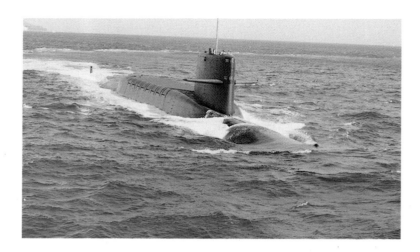

U.S. AND SOVIET NUCLEAR-POWERED BALLISTIC MISSILE SUBMARINES IN SERVICE

U.S. Submarines

Class	In Service	Missile Model/Tubes	Range (Miles)
Ohio	11	Trident I 24	4,600
Lafayette/Franklin	27	Trident I 16	4,600
		Poseidon 16	2,500
TOTAL	38		

Soviet Submarines

Class	In Service	Missile Model/Tubes	Range (Miles)
Typhoon	6	SS-N-20 20	5,100
Delta IV	6	SS-N-23 16	5,100
Delta III	14	SS-N-18 16	4-5,000
Delta II	4	SS-N-8 16	5,600
Delta I	18	SS-N-8 12	5,600
Yankee II	1	SS-N-17 12	2,400
Yankee I	15	SS-N-6 16	1,800
TOTAL	64		

Above: The USS Theodore Roosevelt, a George Washington-class boomer. *Below:* The USS Hawkbill (SSN 666) and the USS Olympia (SSN 717) at rest in the Pearl Harbor Navy Shipyard. Once these hunter/killers are put to sea, Soviet boomers would want to be as far from them as they could get. Similarly, American boomers want to avoid Soviet hunter/killers at all costs.

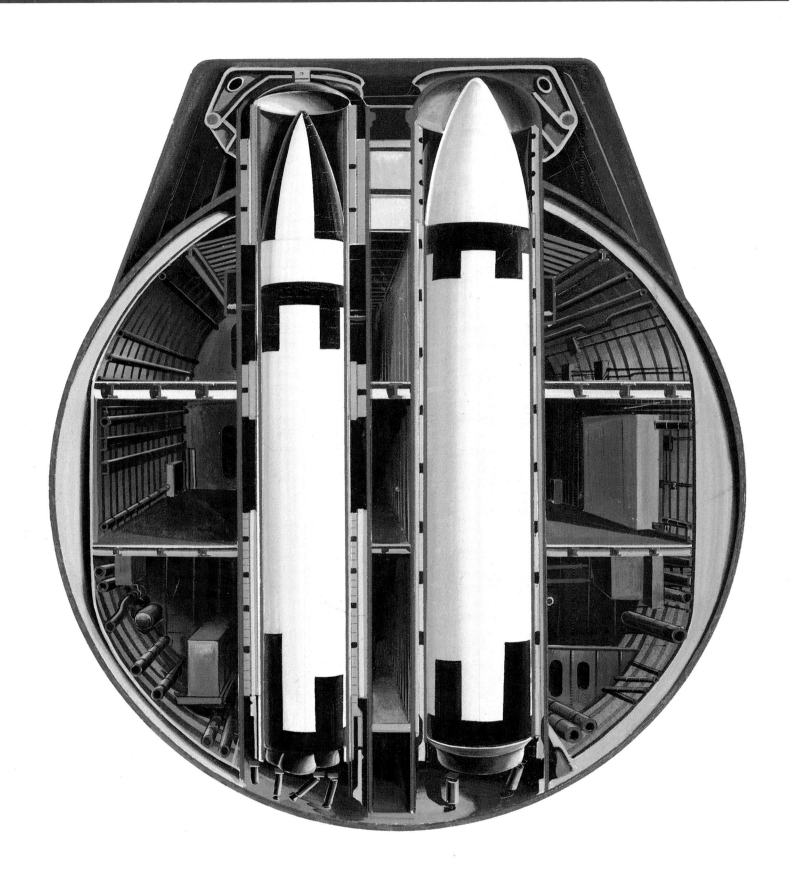

Above: Cross-section of missile tubes on a "generic" boomer, showing a Poseidon C-3 (right) next to a Polaris A-3. In actuality, the two missiles would never have been deployed simultaneously on the same submarine; they appear together here only for the sake of comparison. Earlier variants of the smaller Polaris were the ïirst ballistic missiles to be deployed on U.S. submarines. Although the U.S. Navy has discontinued their use, many remain operational in British service.

Full Page: *The USS* Lafayette *(SSBN 616).* **Insert:** *The USS* Henry M. Jackson *(SSBN 730), a* Lafayette/Franklin-*class boomer.*

Lafayette/Franklin Class.

The first *Lafayette*-class boats were deployed in 1963. Essentially, they are larger and improved versions of the previous *Ethan Allen* boats. They measure 425 feet in length, and are powered by a Westinghouse S5W pressurized water nuclear reactor.

In all, 31 boats were built in this class. The last 12 *Lafayette* boats were modified to such an extent that they are now deemed to be a class of their own, the *Benjamin Franklin* class. *Benjamin Franklin* SSBNs are significantly quieter than *Lafayette* boats.

The first eight *Lafayette* boats carried the 1,730-mile range Polaris A-2 missile, while the rest carried the 2,500-mile range Polaris A-3 with three 300-kiloton nuclear warheads. Between 1970 and 1978, all *Lafayette/Franklin* boats were converted to carry the heavier Poseidon with ten MIRVed warheads and a range of 2,500 miles. Twelve boats were again modified to carry the Trident I (C-4) missile with eight MIRVed warheads and a 4,600-mile range.

All but one of the *Lafayette/Franklin* boats serve with the Atlantic fleet. Three boats have been decommissioned to conform to the Strategic Arms Limitation Treaty (SALT) agreements, one has been converted to a training vessel, and two are scheduled to be removed from active service.

LAFAYETTE/BENJAMIN FRANKLIN-CLASS BALLISTIC MISSILE SUBMARINES

Displacement:	
Surfaced:	7,350 tons
Submerged:	8,250 tons
Dimensions:	
Length:	425 feet
Diameter:	33 feet
Draft:	29 feet
Propulsion:	One S5W pressurized water–cooled nuclear reactor; two geared turbines; one shaft
Speed:	20+ knots (23+ mph)
Maximum diving depth:	984 feet
Armament:	16 Trident I C-4 ballistic missiles (in 12 of the class) 16 Poseidon C-3 ballistic missiles (in 15 of the class) Four 21-inch torpedo tubes (for Mk 48 torpedoes)
Number in service:	27
Crew:	142-147

Right: The USS Henry M. Jackson. *Above:* Sailors man lookout posts on the diving planes of the USS John C. Calhoun *(SSBN 630) as the boat leaves its base in Holy Loch, Scotland.*

Full Page: *The USS* Henry M. Jackson *(SSBN 730).* **Insert:** *The captain and the officer of the deck on the bridge of the USS* Georgia *(SSBN 729).*

Ohio Class.

The boats of this class are the largest SSBNs yet built by the United States. Their length of 560 feet makes them two feet longer than the Soviet *Typhoon*-class boats, but they have a much narrower 42-foot diameter. They also displace 18,750 tons submerged, whereas the *Typhoon* boats may displace as much as 30,000 tons. Driven by a steam turbine that is powered by a General Electric S8G pressurized nuclear reactor, the *Ohio* boats are capable of more than 30 knots submerged and reach depths of up to 1,000 feet. At present their main armament consists of 24 Trident I missiles. At a future date, they are scheduled to be retrofitted with the new Trident II (D-5) missiles.

In addition to the Trident series missiles, the *Ohio* boats are also armed with the Mk 48 21-inch wire-guided heavy torpedo. These weapons are fired from tubes located amidships, and are intended for defensive use against hunter/killer submarines.

The first *Ohio* submarine entered service in October 1982. No official number has ever been given, but it is expected that 20 *Ohio* boomers will be built by the end of the 1990s. These boats are the quietest submarines in the world.

Eleven *Ohio* boats have been built to date. The first ten are deployed with the Pacific fleet, and are based at Bangor, Washington. The Atlantic squadron will be based at Kings Bay, Georgia. A standard tour of duty for the *Ohio* boats includes 70 days on patrol, followed by 25 days in port for replenishment and a minor overhaul. They require a complete overhaul and refueling once every ten years.

OHIO-CLASS BALLISTIC MISSILE SUBMARINES

Displacement:	
Surfaced:	16,765 tons
Submerged:	18,750 tons
Dimensions:	
Length:	560 feet
Diameter:	42 feet
Draft:	36.5 feet
Propulsion:	One S8G natural circulation nuclear reactor; two geared turbines; one shaft
Speed:	30+ knots (35+ mph)
Maximum diving depth:	1,000 feet
Armament:	24 Trident I C-4 ballistic missiles Four 21-inch torpedo tubes (for Mk 48 torpedoes)
Number in service:	11 (four building, two planned)
Crew:	157-160

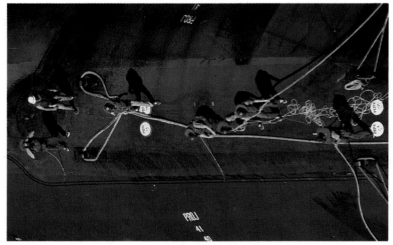

Above: The USS Ohio (SSBN 726), just prior to her naming ceremony in April 1979. *Below:* Line handlers on the USS Nevada *help dock their boat alongside the Explosive Handling Wharf at the submarine base in Bangor, Washington.*

Top Left: A tropical rain shower in no way inhibits the passage of the USS Nevada *(SSBN 733) through the Miraflores lock of the Panama Canal.* **Top Right:** *Line handlers on the deck of the USS* Georgia *(SSBN 729). Note the size of the diving plane extending from the boat's sail.* **Below:** *Rear-angle view of the USS* Ohio *(SSBN 726).*

Right: The USS Alaska *(SSBN 732) next to the submarine tender USS* McKee *(AS 41).* *Below:* An Ohio-class SSBN *heads out to the open sea.*

Left: *The USS* Ohio *in drydock.* **Above:** *The USS* Ohio *before launching.*

Left: Boomers and hunter/killers in various stages of construction in Groton, Connecticut. *Above:* Tugs help in the docking of an Ohio-class boomer.

Right: *The USS* Michigan *in the Magnetic Silencing Facility in Bangor, Washington. The boat is being "degaussed": a process by which electrically charged coils are used to minimize the boat's magnetic signature.* **Above:** *The USS* Ohio *gets underway.*

Opposite: The control room of the USS Georgia *(SSBN 729).* As the diving officer looks on, crewmen operate the wheels that control the boat's diving planes. *Above:* Missile-firing controls in the USS Ohio. *Below:* The control room crew on the USS Ohio prepares for a simulated dive.

Top Right: A crewman on the USS Michigan *(SSBN 727)* exercises by running around the missile compartment in his boat. Nineteen laps equal one mile. *Top Left:* Berthing area for enlisted personnel on the USS Ohio. *Below:* Crew's lounge on the USS Ohio.

Above: Chow time in the mess hall of the USS Ohio. *Bottom Left: A cook prepares rolls for dinner on board the USS* John C. Calhoun. *Bottom Right: Crewmen relaxing in the mess hall of the USS* Andrew Jackson *(SSBN 619).*

U.S. Hunter/killers

As noted earlier, U.S. hunter/killers have been assigned the task of hunting and killing Soviet strategic ballistic missile submarines in the event of war with the Soviet Union. Since the Soviet Navy and merchant marine is in general much smaller than that of the combined NATO forces, American hunter/killers are relieved somewhat of the task, as well as the dangers, of hunting and killing Soviet surface vessels.

Like the Soviet hunter/killers, American SSNs (the designation for nuclear-powered attack submarines) may also be used in a land-attack role. The Soviets have developed a submarine specifically for this role (SSGN). But whereas the Soviets have only recently begun to deploy cruise missiles aboard their SSNs, the U.S. Navy has done so all along. The two principal cruise missile types in the inventory of the U.S. Navy are the Harpoon antiship missile and the Tomahawk long-range antiship or land-attack cruise missile. They were designed to be fired from the 21-inch torpedo tubes that are standard on all torpedo-carrying U.S. submarines. Because they carry a mixed armament, American SSNs are more versatile than Soviet SSNs. Five classes of SSN boats are currently deployed by the U.S. Navy, with a sixth, the *Seawolf* class, still in the design phase. *Seawolf* boats are scheduled to enter service in the mid- to late-1990s.

Right: The USS Providence (SSN 719). *Above: The USS* Cincinnati.

Following the end of World War II, three classes of conventional diesel/electric-powered hunter/killer submarines were built. There were six *Tang*-class boats, three *Barbel*-class boats, and one boat of the *Darter* class. All six *Tang* boats have been discarded, and the last of the *Barbel* boats was decommissioned in 1989. Only the USS *Darter* remains on active service. It is stationed at Sasebo, Japan, and is scheduled for decommissioning in 1990.

The *Nautilus* was the U.S. Navy's first nuclear-powered submarine. Upon its completion in 1954, the *Nautilus* functioned primarily as a research boat, although it was a fully active and capable hunter/killer submarine. The *Nautilus* was decommissioned in March 1980 and is now moored at Groton, Connecticut, as a memorial.

Below: The USS Bonefish, *a diesel/electric hunter/killer of the* Barbel *class. It was decommissioned in 1989.* Opposite Top: *The USS* Nautilus (SSN 571), *the world's first nuclear-powered submarine. At the time it entered service (1954), its unencumbered hull and streamlined sail represented a significant advancement in submarine design.* Opposite Bottom: *Another view of the USS* Nautilus. *The chief service the* Nautilus *performed for the Navy was to acquaint all those concerned with the intricacies of operating a nuclear-powered submarine. But it could have performed as hunter/killer if called upon to do so.*

U.S. AND SOVIET NUCLEAR-POWERED HUNTER/KILLERS IN SERVICE

U.S. Submarines

Class	In Service	Armament
Los Angeles	48	Mk 48/Harpoon/SUBROC Tomahawk
Glenard P. Lipscomb	1	Mk 48/Harpoon/SUBROC Tomahawk
Sturgeon	37	Mk 48/Harpoon/SUBROC Tomahawk
Narwhal	1	Mk 48/Harpoon/Tomahawk
Permit	12	Mk 48/Harpoon/SUBROC
TOTAL	99	

Soviet Submarines

Class	In Service	Armament
Akula	4	SS-N-21 LCM/HT
Mike	Sunk 4/89	
Sierra	1	SS-N-16 AS/HT SS-N-21 LCM/HT
Alfa	6	SS-N-15 AS/HT
Victor III	21	SS-N-16 AS/HT
Victor II	7	SS-N-15 AS/HT
Victor I	16	SS-N-15 AS/HT
Echo	3	SS-N-3 ASM
November	9 (?)	Conventional
TOTAL	67	

NOTE: All Soviet hunter/killers are equipped to fire standard conventional homing torpedoes.
KEY: ASM=Antiship Cruise Missile, AS=Antisubmarine Missile, HT=Conventional homing torpedoes, LCM=Land Attack Cruise Missile

Similar in design to the *Nautilus,* the *Seawolf* was the U.S. Navy's second nuclear-powered submarine. Launched in 1955, the *Seawolf* was destined to be the only submarine of its class. Due to continuing problems with its trouble-prone liquid metal-cooled nuclear reactor, it was retired after only two years of active service. Then, in 1960, the liquid metal-cooled reactor was replaced by a pressurized water-cooled reactor and the *Seawolf* was brought back into service. The *Seawolf* is now in the Pacific fleet reserve.

The *Skate* class was the the U.S. Navy's first class of nuclear-powered hunter/killers to have more than one boat. Four boats of this class were built between December 1957 and December 1959. All have been decommissioned.

The *Skipjack* class boats were built between April 1959 and October 1961. They were the first nuclear-powered submarines in U.S. Navy service that had a streamlined hull for high-speed operations. The *Skipjack* boats could travel at a submerged speed of 30 knots or more. All have been taken out of active service.

U.S. hunter/killer submarines currently in service include the following classes: Permit, Narwhal, Sturgeon, Glenard P. Lipscomb, and Los Angeles.

Opposite Top: The USS Seawolf (SSN 575), the U.S. Navy's second nuclear-powered submarine. Powered by a liquid metal-cooled nuclear reactor when it first entered service in 1955, it was equipped with a less troublesome pressurized water reactor in 1960. *Opposite Bottom:* The USS Skate (SSN 578) and the three boats in its class were similar in design and appearance to the Nautilus and the Seawolf. *Top:* The USS Seadragon (SSN 584), a Skate-*class hunter/killer.* *Bottom Left:* The USS Scamp, a Skipjack-*class hunter/killer.* Skipjack boats were the first U.S. submarines to incorporate the teardrop-shaped hull that is now a standard feature of all modern submarines. In contrast to the older designs, the teardrop shape increases a submarine's submerged speed even as it enhances its maneuverability. *Bottom Right:* The USS Shark (SSN 591), a hunter/killer of the Skipjack *class.*

Above: *The USS* Barb *(SSN 596), a Permit-class hunter/killer.*
Insert: *The* Permit-*class USS* Haddoo *(SSN 604).*

Permit Class.

The 13 boats of this class were commissioned between May 1962 and December 1967. They were designed and built to go fast and dive deep. They can achieve submerged speeds of 30 knots or more. The class was originally named after the USS *Thresher*. It was renamed after the USS *Permit* when *Thresher* was lost in April 1963 while undergoing deep diving trials.

The *Permit* boats are very capable hunter/killers. They are 278 feet long, nearly 32 feet wide, and displace 4,465 tons when submerged. Armament consists of the Harpoon missile, the 21-inch Mk 48 wire-guided heavy torpedo, and the SUBROC anti-submarine missile for distant underwater targets. All submarines of this class except the *Thresher* are still on active duty.

PERMIT-CLASS HUNTER/KILLER SUBMARINES

Displacement:	
Surfaced:	3,750 tons
Submerged:	4,465 tons
Dimensions:	
Length:	278 feet
Diameter:	31.6 feet
Draft:	29 feet
Propulsion:	One S5W pressurized water–cooled nuclear reactor; two steam turbines; one shaft
Speed:	30 knots (35 mph)
Maximum diving depth:	1,300 feet
Armament:	SUBROC missiles Harpoon missiles Mk 48 torpedoes (four tubes)
Number in service:	12
Crew:	127

Right: A tug assists the USS Guardfish *(SSN 612,* Permit *class)* to its mooring in San Diego harbor. *Above:* The Permit-*class* Dace *(SSN 607).*

Pictured: *The USS* Narwhal *(SSN 671).*

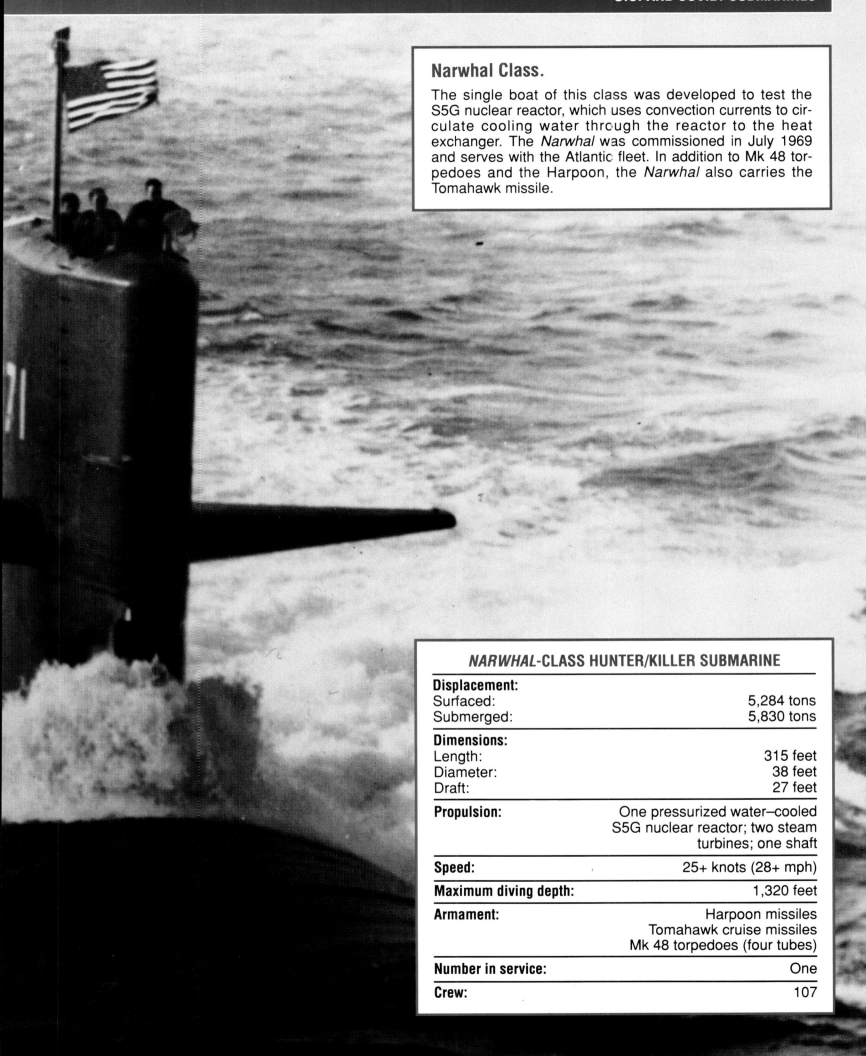

Narwhal Class.

The single boat of this class was developed to test the S5G nuclear reactor, which uses convection currents to circulate cooling water through the reactor to the heat exchanger. The *Narwhal* was commissioned in July 1969 and serves with the Atlantic fleet. In addition to Mk 48 torpedoes and the Harpoon, the *Narwhal* also carries the Tomahawk missile.

NARWHAL-CLASS HUNTER/KILLER SUBMARINE

Displacement:	
Surfaced:	5,284 tons
Submerged:	5,830 tons
Dimensions:	
Length:	315 feet
Diameter:	38 feet
Draft:	27 feet
Propulsion:	One pressurized water–cooled S5G nuclear reactor; two steam turbines; one shaft
Speed:	25+ knots (28+ mph)
Maximum diving depth:	1,320 feet
Armament:	Harpoon missiles Tomahawk cruise missiles Mk 48 torpedoes (four tubes)
Number in service:	One
Crew:	107

Pictured: *Hunter/killers gather in the polar ice. Shown here are the USS* Ray *(SSN 653), the USS* Hawkbill *(SSN 666), and the USS* Archerfish *(SSN 678). All are* Sturgeon-*class boats.*

Sturgeon Class.

This class of hunter/killers was the largest unimproved class of its kind in service with any navy until the advent of the *Los Angeles*-class SSNs. Commissioned between March 1967 and August 1975, the *Sturgeon*-class design corrected most of the deficiencies of its predecessor class, and added an under-the-ice capability as well. All are armed with Mk 48 torpedoes, and Harpoon, Tomahawk, and SUBROC missiles. With their advanced sonar and fire-control systems, the *Sturgeon* boats present a formidable threat to both enemy surface and underwater vessels.

STURGEON-CLASS HUNTER/KILLER SUBMARINES

Displacement:	
Surfaced:	4,460 tons
Submerged:	4,640 tons
Dimensions:	
Length:	292 feet
Diameter:	31.6 feet
Draft:	29 feet
Propulsion:	One S5W pressurized water–cooled nuclear reactor; two steam turbines; one shaft
Speed:	26 knots (30+ mph)
Maximum diving depth:	1,320 feet
Armament:	SUBROC missiles Tomahawk cruise missiles Harpoon missiles Mk 48 torpedoes (four tubes)
Number in service:	37
Crew:	107

Left: *The USS* Bluefish, *a* Sturgeon-*class hunter/killer.*
Above: *The USS* Finback, *a* Sturgeon-*class hunter/killer.*

Right: Evening in San Diego finds the USS Guitarro *(left, SSN 665) and the USS* Haddock *(SSN 621) tethered to their moorings. The* Sturgeon-*class* Guitarro *has a larger sail than the older, smaller,* Permit-*class* Haddock. *Below:* The *Sturgeon-class USS* L. Mendel Rivers *(SSN 686).*

Left and Above: The USS Hammerhead *(SSN 663) (left), and* the USS Hawkbill *(SSN 666).* Sturgeon-*class boats like these two are equipped to carry Tomahawk cruise missiles.* **Top:** *A Tomahawk cruise missile only seconds after launch from a U.S. hunter/killer. Nuclear-tipped cruise missiles can allow hunter/killers to function in a strategic attack role, thus adding to the overall striking power of the Navy's underwater fleet.*

Right: A Tomahawk cruise missile in flight. *Top:* A Tomahawk just after launch from the USS Guitarro. The missile may be fired or "floated" from the boat's 21-inch torpedo tubes. *Above:* A Tomahawk at the instant it makes the transition from undersea weapon to flying missile.

Top, Bottom, and Opposite: Sequence showing a Harpoon antiship missile striking a ship, and the damage done by the weapon. Just as it does with Tomahawk cruise missiles, a hunter/killer launches its Harpoons by firing or floating them out of its torpedo tubes.

Glenard P. Lipscomb Class.

Only a single boat of this class had been built when the decision was reached to build the larger *Los Angeles*-class SSNs instead. A turbine-electric drive that was installed in this boat for evaluation recuced power output and limited speed to 25 knots submerged. The *Lipscomb* is in service with the Atlantic fleet and is armed with Mk 48 torpedoes, and Harpoon, Tomahawk, and SUBROC missiles.

GLENARD P. LIPSCOMB-CLASS HUNTER/KILLER SUBMARINE

Displacement:	
Surfaced:	5,813 tons
Submerged:	6,480 tons
Dimensions:	
Length:	365 feet
Diameter:	32 feet
Draft:	31 feet
Propulsion:	One pressurized water–cooled S5Wa nuclear reactor; turbine–electric drive; one shaft
Speed:	25+ knots (28+ mph)
Maximum diving depth:	1,320 feet
Armament:	SUBROC missiles Tomahawk cruise missiles Harpoon missiles Mk 48 torpedoes (four tubes)
Number in service:	One
Crew:	120

Pictured: The USS Glenard P. Lipscomb *(SSN 685).*

Above: *The* Los Angeles-*class USS* San Francisco *(SSN 711) heads out the channel at Pearl Harbor.* **Insert:** *Bridge crew of the USS* Cincinnati.

Los Angeles Class.

This is the largest class of hunter/killers in the world, and will comprise 66 boats if all planned construction is completed by the mid- to late 1990s. As of this writing, 48 *Los Angeles*-class SSNs are on active service. The first boat, the USS *Los Angeles*, was commissioned in November 1976. All boats in this class are powered by a pressurized water S6G General Electric nuclear reactor that can generate 30,000 hp. Their two steam turbines give them a submerged top speed in excess of 30 knots, and they can dive to a depth of 1,475 feet.

Beginning with the USS *Providence* (SSN 719), it and subsequent boats are referred to as the Improved *Los Angles*-class. These boats are equipped with advanced fire-control and sonar systems, and the Vertical Launch System, which holds 12 Tomahawk missiles in a vertical position. They also have improved under-the-ice capability. Earlier *Los Angeles* boats are equipped with the SUBROC missile. All boats in this class will be refitted with the Mk 117 fire-control system, which will enable them to turn in their SUBROCs for Tomahawk missiles. Additionally, all *Los Angeles* boats carry Mk 48 torpedoes and Harpoon missiles.

The *Los Angeles*-class boats are the premier hunter/killers of the U.S. Navy's submarine fleet, and will likely remain so well into the 21st century.

LOS ANGELES-CLASS HUNTER/KILLER SUBMARINES

Displacement:	
Surfaced:	6,080 tons
Submerged:	6,927 tons
Dimensions:	
Length:	360 feet
Diameter:	33 feet
Draft:	32.3 feet
Propulsion:	One S6G pressurized water–cooled nuclear reactor; two geared turbines; one shaft
Speed:	30+ knots (35+ mph)
Maximum diving depth:	1,475 feet
Armament:	SURBROC missiles Harpoon missiles Twelve vertical launch tubes for Tomahawk cruise missiles Mk 48 torpedoes (four tubes) Mine–laying equipment
Number in service:	48 (12 building, seven planned)
Crew:	127

Left: The USS Atlanta *(SSN 712). The size and turbulence of its wake indicates that it is running under full power.* **Top:** *The USS Salt Lake City (SSN 716).* **Above:** *The USS* Salt Lake City *(SSN 716) in the floating drydock* Arco *in San Diego. Note the* Salt Lake City's *glass-reinforced plastic bow dome, which contains the boat's main sonar equipment.*

Left: The USS Olympia *(SSN 717).* *Above:* Hunter/killers and boomers tied up next to the submarine tender USS Proteus *(AS 19). Submarine tenders can be used to establish a base for submarines in natural harbors with minimal port facilities.* *Top:* The USS Honolulu *(SSN 718) is draped with a traditional (if somewhat oversized) lei as it steams into Pearl Harbor.*

Left: *The USS* Salt Lake City *in the floating drydock* Arco.
Below: *The USS* Salt Lake City *in the floating drydock* Arco *after the water has been pumped out.*

Top: Sailors man the dive planes in the control room of the USS Olympia *(SSN 717).* *Bottom Right:* Crew's washroom on the USS Jacksonville *(SSN 699).* *Bottom Left:* Crew's bunkroom on the USS Portsmouth *(SSN 707).* Although privacy is a rare commodity on board a submarine, the two sailors in the middle bunks have found it by drawing their curtains.

Left: Somewhere deep underwater, crewmen in the control room of the USS Salt Lake City *are engrossed in their respective tasks. Below: Sailors watch a movie in the crew's mess on the USS* Jacksonville.

This Page: *As these three sequential shots demonstrate, an earthen revetment is no protection against the accuracy and explosive force of a hunter/killer-launched Tomahawk cruise missile.* **Opposite Page:** *A Harpoon antiship missile that has been launched from a submerged hunter/killer demonstrates its ship-killing ability in these sequential shots.*

Soviet Boomers

The Soviet Navy was the first to deploy ballistic missile-carrying submarines (also known in the Soviet Union by the acronym PLARBS). Twenty-three of these diesel/electric *Golf*-class boats were built between 1959 and 1966. They carried three SS-N-4 Sark three-stage liquid-fuel missiles, which were 48 feet long and housed in a special compartment that was part of the sail. At least 12 *Golf* boats are thought to be still in service and are collectively designated *Golf II*. They carry the smaller SS-N-5 Serb, which has a range of 805 miles. The *Golf* boats were followed in 1960 by the somewhat more capable diesel/electric boats of the *Hotel*-class. The *Hotel* boats originally carried the SS-N-4, and were later modified (*Hotel II*) to carry the SS-N-5.

Below: Diagram showing relative sizes of U.S. and Soviet boomers. Right: The conventionally powered Soviet Golf I *was the first ballistic missile submarine to enter service in any navy. It carried three missiles in its massive conning tower.*

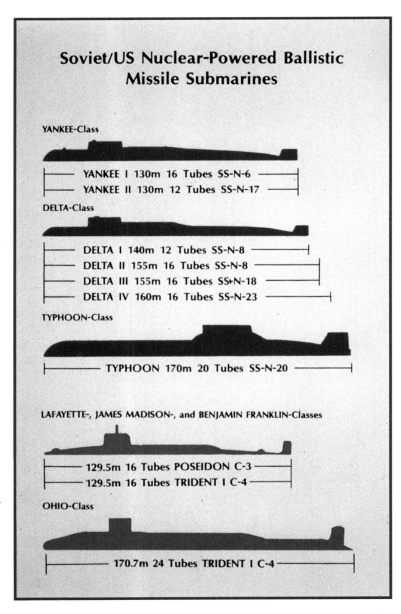

Pictured: *A Soviet* Yankee-*class boomer. Boats of this class were modeled after the U.S.* George Washington- *and* Ethan Allen-*class boomers.* **Insert:** *A Soviet* India-*class rescue submarine. Two deep submergence rescue vehicles are situated in deck wells behind the conning tower. Fires and explosions seem to occur with alarming frequency on the boomers and hunter/killers of the Soviet submarine fleet, thus making the existence of the* India *boats necessary.*

Yankee Class.

In 1966, the Soviets commissioned the first of the *Yankee*-class purpose-built ballistic missile-carrying submarines. These boats were the first Soviet SSBNs to be nuclear powered. Several considerations influenced the design of the *Yankee* boats. First, the SS-N-6 Sawfly solid-fueled ballistic missile was available. Since the latter was significantly smaller and shorter than the SS-N-4 and SS-N-5 used in the *Golf* and *Hotel* boats, the Soviets adopted the American arrangement of 16 missile tubes, eight per side, extending aft of the sail. Because the SS-N-6 had a relatively short 1,800-mile range, *Yankee* boats had to sail across the Atlantic into the coastal waters of North America to get within range of their assigned targets. Since speed was essential to crossing the NATO submarine barriers between Norway and the British Isles and between Greenland, Iceland, and the United Kingdom (GIUK Barrier), *Yankee* submarines were made to cruise at speeds of 27 knots or more. In 1974-75, a *Yankee* boat was modified to fire the newer, longer-range (2,400 miles) SS-N-17. But the SALT agreements prohibited further conversions in this class.

YANKEE-CLASS BALLISTIC MISSILE SUBMARINES

Displacement:	
Surfaced:	7,900 tons
Submerged:	9,600 tons
Dimensions:	
Length:	426 feet
Diameter:	38 feet
Draft:	26 feet
Propulsion:	Two pressurized water–cooled nuclear reactors; two steam turbines; two shafts
Speed:	27 knots (31 mph)
Maximum diving depth:	Not known
Armament:	16 SS-N-17 ballistic missiles (*Yankee I*) 12 SS-N-6 ballistic missiles (*Yankee II*) Six 21-inch torpedo tubes
Number in service:	15 *Yankee I*; one *Yankee II*
Crew:	120

Left: Yankee-*class boomers like this one are designed to cruise at speeds of more than 27 knots.* **Below:** *This Yankee-*class *boomer carries either 12 or 16 ballistic missiles.*

Right: A Yankee-*class boomer.* **Above:** *Early boomers: A Golf II (top) and a* Hotel-*class boomer (above). The boats of these two classes were the first ballistic missile submarines in the Soviet navy. They were all conventionally powered.*

ured: *A Delta IV. The hunchbacked configuration is a ctive feature of all boats in this class.*

Delta Class.

Needing a more capable ballistic missile submarine, the Soviet Navy began deploying the *Delta*-class boats in 1972. Four *Delta* variations have been identified to date and construction is still underway within this classification. All four variations are thought to be driven by the same pressurized water-cooled nuclear reactors, which enable them to achieve speeds in excess of 24 knots. The *Delta I* boats carried 12 SS-N-8, Modification (MOD) 1 missiles with ranges of 4,800 miles. (A subsequent modification of the SS-N-8 enabled this missile to achieve a range of 5,600 miles.) Because the SS-N-8 is quite a bit larger than the SS-N-6, it has a more spacious missile compartment behind the sail. The resulting hunchbacked shape of the missile compartment is a distinctive characteristic of the *Delta I* boats. The *Delta II* hull was lengthened by 30 feet to hold four additional missiles.
Continued on page 139.

DELTA-CLASS BALLISTIC MISSILE SUBMARINES

Displacement:	*Delta I*: 9,000 tons surfaced, 11,750 tons submerged *Delta II*: 10,000 tons surfaced, 12,750 submerged *Delta III*: 10,500 tons surfaced, 13,250 submerged *Delta IV*: 10,800 tons surfaced, 13,500 submerged
Dimensions:	*Delta I*: length, 459 feet; diameter, 39 feet; draft, 29 feet *Delta II/III*: length, 508 feet; diameter 39 feet; draft, 29 feet *Delta IV*: length, 544 feet; diameter, 39 feet; draft, 29 feet
Propulsion:	All models: Two pressurized water–cooled nuclear reactors; two steam turbines; two shafts
Speed:	All models: 25 knots (29 mph)
Maximum diving depth:	Not known
Armament:	*Delta I*: 12 SS-N-8 ballistic missiles *Delta II*: 16 SS-N-8 ballistic missiles *Delta III*: 16 SS-N-18 ballistic missiles *Delta IV*: 16 SS-N-23 ballistic missiles All models: six 21-inch torpedo tubes
Number in service:	*Delta I,* 18; *Delta II,* 4; *Delta III,* 14; *Delta IV,* 6
Crew:	All models: 120

Delta Class continued.

The *Delta III* was similar in design and construction to the previous *I* and *II* models, but with a missile compartment built eight feet higher to hold the new SS-N-18 Stingray ballistic missile. The SS-N-18 had a range of between 4,000 and 5,000 miles, depending on its payload. It was 46 feet long, some four feet longer than the SS-N-8. It also carried a new MIRVed triple warhead. Some *Delta III* boats are also thought to be equipped with the SS-N-18 Mod 3, which has seven MIRVed warheads.

The *Delta IV* series also has a higher missile compartment that reaches nearly to the top of the sail. Aft stabilizers were added to cope with the increased height of the compartment. It carries the newest Soviet sea-to-land ballistic missile, the SS-N-23. The SS-N-23 has a range of 4,150 miles and carries ten MIRVed warheads.

Left: A Delta II *shows off its unique profile.* *Above:* Port bow shot of a Delta II.

139

Right: The stepped configuration of its missile compartment indicates that this submarine is a Delta I. *In later* Delta *variants the missile compartment angled straight down to the deck without an interim step.* *Above:* *Another view of a* Delta I. *All* Delta *boats were designed to take advantage of progressive advancements in Soviet missile technology.*

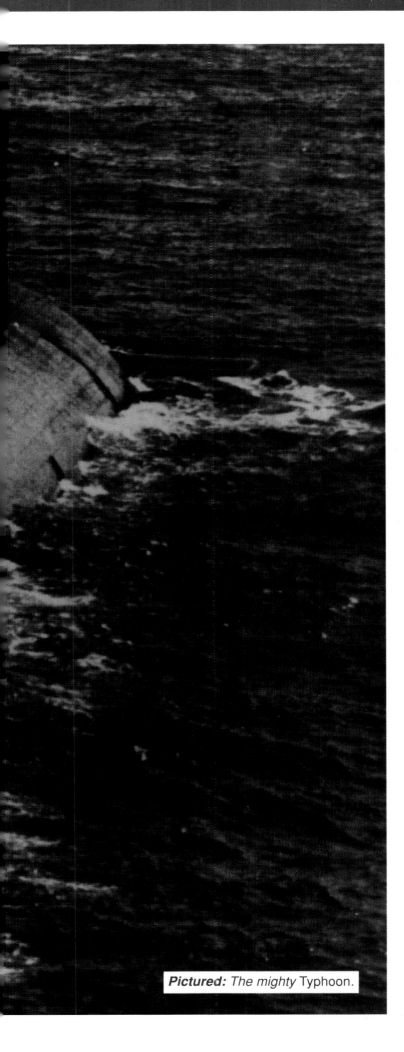

Pictured: *The mighty* Typhoon.

Typhoon Class.

With the development of the ong-range, MIRVed SS-N-23 and SS-N-20 ballistic missiles, Soviet SSBN tactics began to change. Now it was no longer necessary to run the gauntlet of NATO, U.S./Canadian, or U.S./Japanese ASW defenses to reach their patrol stations off the North American continent. Instead Soviet SSBNs could use the concealment of the Arctic ice pack, which they could reach quickly and easily from their northern bases. Or, they could remain in home-coastal waters and still be within striking distance of their targets.

The *Typhoon*-class submarines were custom designed and built to fully exploit the capabilities of the new missiles. Measuring 558 feet from bow to stern and 75 feet in diameter, the boats of the *Typhoon* class are the largest submarines in the world. They are the same length, but twice the width and nearly twice the displacement weight of the American *Ohio*-class boomers. Their armament consists of 20 5,100-mile range SS-N-20 ballistic missiles, which are stored in 20 launchers forward of the sails. Each SS-N-20 carries 10 MIRVed warheads. The sails on these boats are reinforced for punching through the Arctic ice pack to launch their missiles.

The *Typhoon* boats are powered by nuclear reactor-driven steam turbines, which enable them to achieve submerged speeds in excess of the publicly admitted 24 knots. Because their power plants are extraordinarily quiet, the *Typhoon* boats are nearly undetectable. However, their great size does have its limitations: Specialized facilities for their construction, which exist only at the Severodvinsk shipyards, are capable of producing only two *Typhoon* boats per year.

TYPHOON-CLASS BALLISTIC MISSILE SUBMARINES

Displacement:	
Surfaced:	18,500 tons
Submerged:	26,000-30,000 tons
Dimensions:	
Length:	558 feet
Diameter:	75 feet
Draft:	43 feet
Propulsion:	Two pressurized water–cooled nuclear reactors; two steam turbines; two shafts
Speed:	27 knots (31 mph)
Maximum diving depth:	Not known
Armament:	20 SS-N-20 ballistic missiles Six 21-inch torpedo tubes, four 16-inch tubes
Number in service:	Six
Crew:	150

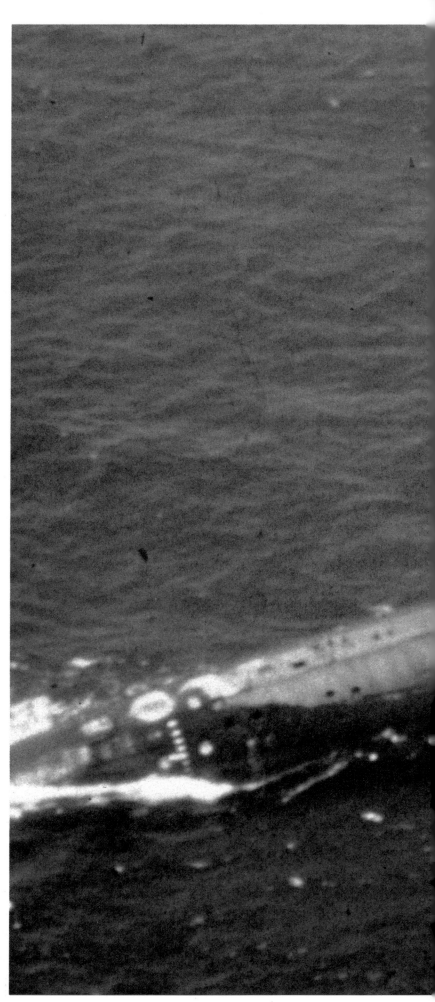

Above and Right: Cruise missile submarines like this Charlie-class boat (right) and the Oscar-class boat (above) are meant to augment the striking power of the Soviets' ballistic missile submarine fleet. Boats of both classes are nuclear powered. In the U.S. Navy, hunter/killers are equipped to function as cruise missile-launching submarines.

Soviet Hunter/killers

The Soviets have developed a wide variety of conventional and nuclear-powered hunter/killer submarines. The conventionally powered boats operate primarily in coastal areas and inland waterways such as the Black and Baltic seas. The nuclear-powered boats discussed here operate throughout the world's oceans.

Below: A November-*class hunter/killer off the west coast of Ireland in 1970. When this photo was taken, the boat was on the verge of foundering. It later sank from unknown causes. Right: An* Echo II *cruise missile submarine. The four dark indentations on each side of the hull serve as blast deflectors for the missile-launching tubes immediately in front of them.*

November Class.

The *November*-class submarines were the first nuclear-powered hunter/killers in the Soviet Navy. One sank off the Spanish Atlantic coast in 1970 and at least two others have been withdrawn from service. Of the original 12 boats, therefore, only nine remain in service, and at least two of these may have been relegated to the reserve fleet. They are known to have both 16-inch and 21-inch torpedo tubes, and could possibly be equipped with the SS-N-15 and SS-N-16 nuclear-tipped antisubmarine missiles. But in all probability, they are armed with conventional homing torpedoes.

NOVEMBER-CLASS BALLISTIC MISSILE SUBMARINES	
Displacement:	
Surfaced:	4,500 tons
Submerged:	5,300 tons
Dimensions:	
Length:	361 feet
Diameter:	30 feet
Draft:	25 feet
Propulsion:	Two pressurized water–cooled nuclear reactors; two steam turbines; two shafts
Speed:	30 knots (35 mph)
Maximum diving depth:	Not known
Armament:	Conventional homing torpedoes (eight 21-inch tubes)
Number in service:	Nine (?)
Crew:	80

Echo Class.

The five boats in this class were originally built to be cruise missile-launching submarines (SSGN). They were converted into hunter/killers starting in 1968. Only three remain in service.

ECHO-CLASS HUNTER/KILLER SUBMARINES

Displacement:	
Surfaced:	4,600 tons
Submerged:	5,400 tons
Dimensions:	
Length:	361 feet
Diameter:	30 feet
Draft:	25 feet
Propulsion:	Two pressurized water–cooled nuclear reactors; two steam turbines; two shafts
Speed:	28 knots (32 mph)
Maximum diving depth:	Not known
Armament:	SS-N-3 antiship missiles Conventional homing torpedoes (six 21-inch tubes, four 16-inch tubes)
Number in service:	Three
Crew:	75

Pictured: *This Victor III has a longer bow section than its predecessors. It also has improved sensors and larger torpedo tubes.*

Victor Class.

Prior to 1960, Soviet hunter/killer operations were confined to Soviet coastal waters and choke points approaching the Soviet Union. But when the United States began deploying the *George Washington*-class SSBNs in 1960, the Soviets changed their tactics. Using *Victor*-class boats that were equipped with the most sophisticated sonar equipment then available, they instead began to patrol in North American coastal waters. There, the Soviet hunter/killers lay in wait for American boomers leaving port, and then attempted to shadow their adversaries as the latter moved to their patrol areas. The purpose of this exercise was two-fold: first, to discover the approximate areas that American boomers frequented; second, to develop a data base of sonar signals and other characteristics whereby American submarines could be identified. When this tactic proved to be a failure, the Soviet hunter/killers were reassigned to escort and guardian service for their own boomers.
Continued on page 150.

VICTOR-CLASS HUNTER/KILLER SUBMARINES

Displacement:	*Victor I*: 4,300 tons surfaced, 5,100 tons submerged *Victor II*: 4,500 tons surfaced, 5,700 tons submerged *Victor III*: 4,800 tons surfaced, 6,000 tons submerged
Dimensions:	*Victor I*: length, 308 feet; diameter, 34 feet; draft, 24 feet *Victor II*: length, 338 feet; diameter, 34 feet; draft, 24 feet *Victor III*: length, 351 feet; diameter, 34 feet; draft 24 feet
Propulsion:	All models: two pressurized water–cooled nuclear reactors; one steam turbine; one shaft
Speed:	30-32 knots (35-36 mph)
Maximum diving depth:	Not known
Armament:	*Victor I/II*: SS-N-15 antisubmarine missiles *Victor III*: SS-N-16 antisubmarine missiles All models: conventional homing torpedoes (*Victor I/II*, six 21-inch tubes; *Victor III*, two 21-inch, four 25.6-inch tubes)
Number in service:	*Victor I*, 16; *Victor II*, 7; *Victor III*, 21;
Crew:	90-100

Victor Class continued.
The *Victor I* and *Victor II* boats are both armed with the SS-N-15 nuclear-tipped missiles, although they can certainly carry non-nuclear homing torpedoes as well. The *Victor III* boats carry the SS-N-16 missile, which is a wider, more capable antisubmarine weapon than its predecessor. The *Victor III* boats can also carry the Type 65 homing torpedo for use against surface ships. The Type 65 can chase a surface vessel for more than 30 miles at a 40-knot speed. The most identifiable feature of a *Victor III* boat is the pod atop its vertical tail. The pod is thought to house a towed passive sonar array. The *Victor* class is being replaced by the *Akula* class.

Right: Conning tower of a Victor II. *Below: Bird's-eye-view of a* Victor I *hunter/killer. Bottom: A* Victor II *approaches the camera head-on.*

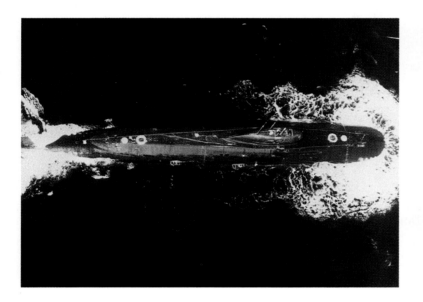

Alfa Class.

The boats of this class were built in the 1960s and early 1970s. Their design incorporated many of that era's most advanced attack submarine technologies. Exceptionally fast at 45 knots or more, they are capable of diving to depths no other submarine can match. Reliable reports have them achieving operational depths of 1,970 feet, with a maximum diving depth of 2,950 feet.

In order to achieve such depths, the Soviets developed a whole new technology for fabricating and welding the titanium pressure hulls of the *Alfa* boats. These hulls made possible operations at levels that are beyond the reach of homing torpedoes. At shallower depths, the ruggedness of their titanium hulls makes the *Alfa* boats hard to destroy with conventional weapons of all types.

The *Alfa* boats first went to sea in 1972. They are driven by a compact but quite noisy liquid metal-cooled nuclear reactor. Legend has it that when the first *Alfa* boat entered the Bering Sea on its maiden voyage, it was heard by sensors as far south as Newport News, Virginia. Improvements have been made to quiet the boat, but it is still very noisy by modern standards. Equipped with six torpedo tubes, the Alfa boats can carry SS-N-15 missiles as well as conventional torpedoes. The boats of this class are too small to hold the larger SS-N-16 missile. The Soviet nickname for the *Alfa* boats is *zolotaya ryba*, or "golden fish"—an ironic reference to their exceptionally high production costs.

ALFA-CLASS HUNTER/KILLER SUBMARINES

Displacement:	
Surfaced:	2,900 tons
Submerged:	3,680 tons
Dimensions:	
Length:	267 feet
Diameter:	31 feet
Draft:	23 feet
Propulsion:	Two liquid metal-cooled nuclear reactors; two steam turbo-alternators, one motor, turbo-electric; one shaft
Speed:	45 knots (51 mph)
Maximum diving depth:	2,950 feet (estimated)
Armament:	SS-N-15 antisubmarine missiles Conventional homing torpedoes (six 21-inch tubes)
Number in service:	Six
Crew:	40

Pictured: An Alfa-*class hunter/killer. Although* Alfa *boats incorporate many advanced features in their design, they have been plagued by problems that have diminished their overall effectiveness.*

Sierra Class.

The design of the *Sierra*-class boats represents a marked improvement over the *Alfa*-class boat design. Like the *Alfa* boats, the *Sierra* boats have titanium hulls; however, these boats also feature the traditional double-hulled construction of older-model Soviet submarines. But the most distinctive feature of the *Sierra* boats is the teardrop-shaped pod mounted horizontally on the tail fin. No one in the West knows what this pod is for. Some believe that it houses a device for increasing stability, others that it shields a separate motor for silent running. Such a motor is thought to work by using a magnetic field to influence a flexible, double-walled hollow tube filled with a fluid containing metal particles. The fluid would be influenced by the magnetic field, which, when pulsed, would cause the tube to flex—thus pumping water silently and propulsively.

The *Sierra* boats are armed with SS-N-16 antisubmarine torpedoes, conventional torpedoes, and probably SS-N-21 land-attack cruise missiles. The SS-N-21 is somewhat similar to the U.S. Tomahawk. To date, only one submarine in this class is known to be operational.

SIERRA-CLASS HUNTER/KILLER SUBMARINE	
Displacement:	
Surfaced:	6,000 tons
Submerged:	7,550tons
Dimensions:	
Length:	360 feet
Diameter:	39 feet
Draft:	25 feet
Propulsion:	Two nuclear reactors, either pressurized water- or liquid metal-cooled; two turbo alternators; one shaft
Speed:	34 knots (39 mph)
Maximum diving depth:	Not known
Armament:	SS-N-16 antisubmarine missiles SS-N-21 cruise missiles Conventional homing torpedoes (six 21-inch and 25.6-inch tubes)
Number in service:	One
Crew:	100

Above: A Sierra-*class hunter/killer. The pod on the tail fin may contain a stabilizing device, or a quiet propulsion system. Insert: Aerial view of a* Sierra-*class boat.*

Mike Class.

The single boat in this class of hunter/killer submarine was essentially a quieter version of an *Alfa* boat. It too had a titanium pressure hull, but was also double-hulled in the traditional Russian manner. It was the largest hunter/killer submarine in the world, measuring forty more feet in length, six more feet in width, and displacing 2,773 more tons of water when submerged than the SSN boats of the U.S. *Los Angeles*-class. Little is known about the *Mike*-class. Commissioned in 1983, the first and only boat so far sank after catching fire in the Norwegian Sea in April 1989. It had 16- and 25.6-inch torpedo tubes for the SS-N-15 and SS-N-16 missiles, and may have been armed with SS-N-21 land-attack cruise missiles as well.

MIKE-CLASS HUNTER/KILLER SUBMARINES

Displacement:	
Surfaced:	6,400 tons
Submerged:	8,000 tons
Dimensions:	
Length:	360 feet
Diameter:	39 feet
Draft:	30 feet
Propulsion:	Two liquid metal–cooled nuclear reactors; two turbo alternators; one shaft
Speed:	26 knots (30 mph)
Maximum diving depth:	Not known
Armament:	SS-N-15 antisubmarine missiles SS-N-21 cruise missiles Conventional homing torpedoes (six 21-inch and 25.6-inch tubes)
Number in service:	0 (single *Mike* boat sunk 4/89)
Crew:	70

Pictured: This Mike-*class boat was the only submarine of its kind. It was the largest hunter/killer in the world until an electrical fire caused it to sink in the Barents Sea in April 1989.*

Pictured: *An aptly-named Akula (shark)-class boat. The quietness of the Akula boats is a source of much concern to Western naval strategists.*

Akula Class.

Very little is known about this new class of hunter/killer submarine. The first boat was commissioned in 1988 and is thought to have finished its sea trials in mid- to late 1989. Like the boats of the *Alfa* and *Mike* classes, the *Akula* ("shark") has a titanium pressure hull. Photographs of the *Akula* running on the surface show drain ports in the hull, which are normally associated with a double-hull construction. The Akula also has the peculiar teardrop-shaped pod mounted atop its vertical fin that is seen on the *Sierra*-class boats. Much to the surprise of Western observers, *Akula* boats were extremely quiet in comparison to the previous Soviet class nuclear-powered hunter/killers. When they entered service, the Soviets were thought to be incapable of constructing boats this quiet for at least another five years. It is not currently known if additional *Akula* boats will be built.

AKULA-CLASS HUNTER/KILLER SUBMARINES

Displacement:	
Surfaced:	7,500 tons
Submerged:	9,000 tons
Dimensions:	
Length:	371 feet
Diameter:	43 feet
Draft:	33 feet
Propulsion:	Two pressurized water–cooled nuclear reactors; two steam turbines; one shaft
Speed:	32 knots (37 mph)
Maximum diving depth:	Not known
Armament:	SS-N-21 antisubmarine missiles Conventional homing torpedoes (six 21-inch and 25.6-inch tubes)
Number in service:	Four
Crew:	90

Additional Submarine Forces

As mentioned earlier, other nations besides the U.S. and the Soviet Union currently deploy submarine forces. For instance, France has developed and deployed an all-nuclear submarine force similar to that of the United States. It has two strategic ballistic missile classes, the oldest of which are the five submarines of the *Le Redoubtable* class (1971). These boats are armed with 16 MSBS M-20 single-warhead missiles, each with a range of 2,140 miles. The boats of the new *L'Inflexible* class carry 16 MSBS M-4 missiles with six warheads each and ranges of 2,500 miles. Only one boat of this class has been built to date.

France also deploys a single class of hunter/killer submarines, the *Rubris* class (1982). The construction program for the five boats to be built in this class is scheduled for completion in the early 1990s. The *Rubris* class is thought to be powered by a compact nuclear reactor using a liquid metal coolant.

Great Britain has built four SSBNs of the *Resolution* class (1967). Each boat carries 16 Polaris A-3 ballistic missiles, which have ranges of 2,875 miles and come equipped with British-built MIRV triple warheads.

Right: The Saphir, *a hunter/killer of the French* Rubis *class.*
Above: The Redoubtable, *name-ship of the French* Le Redoubtable *class of boomers.*

Great Britain has deployed three classes of nuclear-powered hunter/killer submarines. These include the five boats of the *Valiant* class (1966); the six boats of the *Swiftsure* class (1973); and seven planned boats of the *Trafalgar* class (1983). Great Britain is also adding the diesel/electric-powered *Upholder* class (1988), for which ten boats are planned. To the Royal Navy's submarine service goes the unique distinction of having used a nuclear-powered hunter/killer to sink an enemy ship in actual combat. The incident occurred during the 1982 Falklands Island War, when the *Valiant*-class submarine HMS *Conqueror* sank the Argentinean cruiser *General Belgrano*.

The world's fifth-largest nuclear-powered submarine fleet belongs to the People's Republic of China. Its *Xia* class SSBNs (1985) carry 12 CSS-N-4 single warhead ballistic missiles with ranges of 2,500 miles. Two such boats have been built and deployed to date. All Chinese hunter/killers are powered by conventional means.

Other navies, most notably that of West Germany, Sweden, and India, deploy a number of hunter/killer submarines. To date, none of them are nuclear powered.

Left: The Rubis, *name-ship of the French* Rubis-*class of hunter/killers. The fact that the* Rubis *boats are the smallest nuclear-powered hunter/killers in any navy has led naval experts of other countries to believe that its reactor design is highly innovative. Above: A British* Valiant-*class hunter/killer. Boats of this class were the first nuclear submarines designed solely by the British. Their primary mission is to protect task forces and convoys from hostile hunter/killers.*

STALKING ARMAGEDDON: A SCENARIO FOR UNDERSEA WARFARE

With the Soviet system in turmoil, Soviet leaders may one day resort to military action as a way of resolving their problems. If that day ever comes, here's how it might be spent by the submariners of both sides....

Deep, black, cold. The water temperature is four degrees Celsius at a depth of 1,000 feet. There is no light, no sound, no odor.

A shape materializes, and glides past with scarcely a ripple to mark its passage. Behind the slowly turning screw that propels it there is only a slight disturbance in the water.

The shape, a Soviet strategic ballistic missile submarine, is moving southwest on an underwater heading of 207 degrees after making a long, sweeping turn out of the ice-covered Barents Sea. The turn has taken it to the north and west of the NATO submarine patrol area that extends from the North Cape of Norway toward the northern tip of Greenland.

Pictured: *The USS* Cincinnati *sails into the sunset at the beginning of its patrol. The hunt for Soviet submarines will begin as soon as it submerges.*

00 Hours Zulu: The Boomer

The Soviet commander of the *Typhoon*-class submarine *Liberation,* a Captain of the First Rank, was confident that he had slipped past the NATO antisubmarine warfare (ASW) defenses that lay between the coast of Norway and Great Britain. This far-flung net of underwater sensors works in conjunction with NATO nuclear-powered and conventional diesel/electric attack submarines, as well as constantly patrolling surface vessels and long-range ASW aircraft, to form a barrier that extends clear across the North Atlantic to Iceland. Getting through it without incident had

been quite an accomplishment, and the captain was accordingly proud of himself and his crew.

As formidable as it was, however, this barrier paled in comparison to the main line of NATO ASW defenses that stretched across the Denmark Strait, which lay nearly 600 miles to the south of the *Liberation*'s present position. It was altogether logical for NATO to heavily guard the Denmark Strait, inasmuch as it forms a seagoing passage between Iceland and Greenland, and points the way to the east coasts of the United States and Canada. And because it does lead to the North American continent, the

strait represents an equally logical route for a Soviet submarine to transit. But the captain of the *Liberation* had no intention of trying to run that gauntlet.

His vessel was a strategic ballistic missile submarine, or "boomer," as it was called by his enemies in the West. It was armed with a total of 200 nuclear warheads, which were carried in MIRVed packets of ten on the boat's full complement of 20 SS-N-20 5,100-mile range ballistic missiles. The warheads were earmarked for targets as far south as Houston, and as far inland as Kansas City. As matters now stood, the Soviet high command had not yet decided to launch these missiles. But the hour of confrontation with the West was drawing nigh, and the Soviets wanted to be ready. To that end, they had ordered the Soviet captain to take his boat just inside the Denmark Strait, to an area at the edge of the polar ice pack known as the marginal sea ice zone (MIZ). Here he would lie low and await an ELF (extremely low frequency) signal bearing further instructions. While he remained stationary, two additional *Typhoon*-class boats and two *Delta IV*-class boats would attempt to penetrate the strait, and thereby decoy American and Canadian ASW efforts away from the *Liberation*.

Left: The USS Queenfish *(SSN 651) near the North Pole. It occupies a hole in the ice that the Soviets would call a "polynya." Above: This sonar-dipping SH-60F Seahawk represents the kind of ASW activity a Soviet submarine might expect to find while attempting a submerged transit of the Denmark Strait.*

01:00 Hours Zulu: The Hunter/killer

In the brightly lit control room of the USS *Denver,* an American captain was waiting for a computer to identify the noise his boat's bow-mounted sonar had just detected. The USS *Denver* was an SSN, a nuclear-powered attack submarine, or hunter/killer, of the *Los Angeles* class. Its prey was enemy submarines, and like all efficient predators, it was adept at the art of silently stalking whatever it intended to kill.

An hour earlier, while the *Denver* was making its way to a patrol station off the Norwegian coast, the boat's WLR-9 passive sonar receiver had indicated that another submarine might be in the area. Under normal circumstances, the captain would have ignored the blip as an aberration

caused by varying degrees of salinity, conflicting currents, or differing temperature levels. But with the threat of war looming in Eastern Europe, he had thought it best to bring his boat to dead slow ahead for the purpose of investigating the source of the blip. Then, after thirty minutes without an incoming sound, he had ordered the boat ahead at five knots and had put out the BQR-15 towed array passive receiver. Whereupon, after a brief interval, his sonar operator had picked up a second suspicious sound. This was the sound that the computer was still processing for identification.

A few seconds later, the chief sonar operator informed the captain that the computer had identified the submarine as the *Liberation,* a boat that belonged to the newest class of Soviet nuclear-powered boomers.

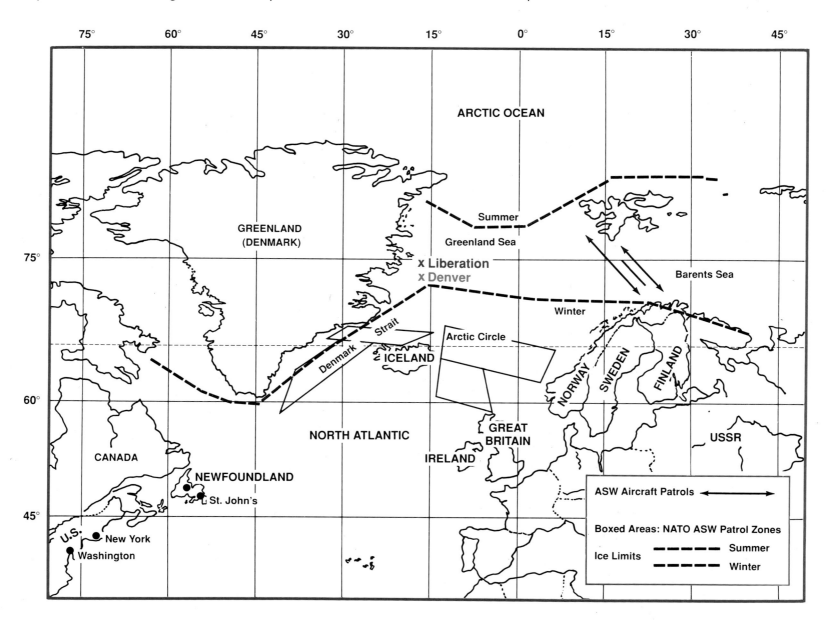

It was immediately evident to the American captain that his Soviet counterpart had positioned his submarine well. The *Liberation* was in an area where the Arctic surface and deep water masses butt against the shallow, intermediate, and deep and bottom waters of the North Atlantic. Here, temperature, currents, and the amount of salt in the water could create areas that were alternately transparent and opaque to sonar. Moreover, the movement of icebergs as they broke away from the polar ice pack and collided with each other created a great deal of noise that could only confuse the issue. In these conditions, sonar might show the Soviet boat to be as distant as fifty miles, or as close as fifty feet.

All this notwithstanding, the chief sonar operator was able to snatch a faint trace of identifiable sound from the bliz-zard of background noise. In this he was aided by sophisti-cated sonar technology, his own skill, and not a little luck. He guessed that the sound, weak as it was, emanated from the Soviet boat's active under-ice sonar.

When the navigation officer plotted the bearing of the sig-nal—155 degrees true—he discovered that the *Liberation's* course more or less intersected the Greenland coast. Dis-tressed by this news, the captain made a rough plot of pos-sible targets for the *Liberation's* missiles. Using a map and a set of dividers, he quickly proved to his own satisfac-tion—and dismay—that the Soviet missiles were capable of visiting nuclear Armageddon on the entire East Coast, as well as half the midwestern regions of Canada and the United States.

Left: Map showing approximate locations of the USS Denver *and the Soviet* Typhoon-*class* Liberation. *Above: Overhead view of the bridge of the USS* Salt Lake City.

06:00 Hours Zulu: The Boomer Threat

Like all good submarine captains, the Soviet captain was a patient man. He understood that the sea is timeless and vast, and that move and countermove rarely go according to plan. The captain was also a patriot; he loved his country and was grateful for the opportunities it had afforded him. And like many Soviet citizens he had watched first with skepticism, then with trepidation, as social and political changes had swept across the Soviet Union in the late 1980s. Democratic reforms had charged forward at breakneck speed, and before anyone realized what had happened, the nations of the Warsaw Pact had ceased to be Communist. Almost overnight, it seemed, the buffer that had existed between the *Rodina,* the motherland, and the West had vanished.

Once the tide of liberal reform had abated—as it always did in Russia—the conservatives had returned to power stronger than before. They had attempted to reassert Soviet military dominance over Eastern Europe, only to discover that the nations and peoples that had once been so submissive to their rule were now unwilling to revert to the former status quo. This was especially true in Czechoslovakia, where anti-Soviet sentiment increasingly found expression in abusive behavior toward Soviet nationals. At first limited to hissed curses and whispered threats, such abuse quickly turned violent. On the streets of Prague, fistfights between Soviet troops and Czech youths became commonplace occurrences, as did the pelting of moving Soviet automobiles with beer bottles and stones. When a Soviet diplomat was savagely beaten by a mob in Wenceslaus Square, it was decided in the Kremlin that the limits of

Left and Above: In August 1968 Soviet tanks entered Prague to quell an incipient uprising. Some 21 years later, mass demonstrations in Prague's Wenceslaus Square signaled the beginning of the end of Communism in Czechoslovakia. Both events were examples of the kind of turmoil that could, at some future date, provoke a military response by hardliners in the Soviet leadership.

tolerance had been reached. Soviet forces encamped in the Czechoslovakian countryside were mobilized forthwith, and tanks were ordered into Prague itself.

In response, anti-communist riots promptly flared up all over the country, with militant sympathizers pouring in from Poland, East Germany, and Hungary to lend assistance to the rebellious Czechs. The rioting turned to fierce street-fighting and the Czechoslovakian Army struck hard at the

Soviets. Several pitched battles were fought, and Soviet tanks and troops were forced to retreat into the Ukraine. In a flash, sympathetic demonstrations against the Soviet Union erupted in all the Warsaw Pact nations. Desperate to reverse the dissolution of the East Bloc, the Kremlin prepared a massive counterthrust from the Ukraine.

Western reaction to these events had been predictable enough: NATO had vacillated on the nature of the support

it would offer Czechoslovakia and Poland, whereupon the President of the United States had unconditionally guaranteed the integrity of the Czech and Polish borders. The President had announced his guarantee on a worldwide television hookup that had carried his broadcast into the Soviet Union. He thought he had drawn a line the Soviets would not dare to cross, but in this the Soviets seemed bound and determined to prove him wrong—even at the risk of precipitating a planetary cataclysm.

Thus, in less than a month the Cold War had been renewed, filled with the menace of major superpower conflict. All over the world, armies were on the march and warships were putting to sea in anticipation of war. If and when that war started, the *Liberation*'s mission was terrifyingly simple: It was to render the United States incapable of launching its intercontinental ballistic missiles by performing a decapitating strike against American missile bases and command centers.

Left: A column of Soviet tanks rumbles down a side street near Old Town Square in Prague in August 1968. More recently, the Soviets used armor to crush paramilitary forces in Azerbaijan in January 1990. Such tactics may become more common as Moscow seeks to assert its ever-weakening authority over the rebellious nations of its crumbling empire.

06:00 Hours Zulu: The Hunt Begins

At less than five knots, the USS *Denver* felt its way along the bearing established earlier. All aboard hoped that the boat's two sonar systems—the forward-looking set mounted on the bow, and the passive array being towed behind—would be able to snatch another sound from the incessant rumbling and screeching that gained steadily in intensity as it approached the MIZ.

The American captain suspected that the *Liberation* was somewhere near the ice edge. In all likelihood, the Soviet boat would be situated beneath a *polynya*, perhaps with an antenna thrust up through the ice waiting for a message from its command authority. Either that, or it would be hovering deep below the ice.

The *Denver's* captain wanted to inform his superiors in Portsmouth that his boat was tracking a Soviet boomer.

But two considerations stayed his hand in this regard. The first involved the possibility of detection by Soviet satellites or surveillance aircraft. To transmit a message he would have to approach the surface and release a communications buoy, which would send a signal containing his message to a communications relay satellite. The signal would almost certainly be intercepted by the Soviets, who could only conclude that it had come from an American attack submarine that was tracking one of their boomers.

The second consideration involved the possibility of drawing too much friendly attention to the area. If CNCLANT-FLT (Commander-in-Chief, Atlantic Fleet) organized an intensive ASW effort hereabouts, that too would alert the Soviet boat and drive it even deeper into hiding. The American captain therefore decided against informing Portsmouth of his activities. Right now, he was in the driver's seat—he knew the Soviet boomer was out there, but the boomer did not know he knew. He hoped.

Left: With diving planes rotated to the vertical position, the USS Whale *surfaces through the polar ice.* *Above:* A sonar operator with his headphones on listens for any out-of-the-ordinary noises. Sonar operators in U.S. submarines are engaged in a constant search for Soviet boats.

10:45 Hours Zulu: Alert

The Soviet captain heard the bell ring inside the communications cabin. Two minutes later, he was handed a decoded transmission. Below the time and date notation and the code for his boat, was the simple message: "Alert 2."

Alert 2 told the captain that the international situation was worsening and that war was imminent. That meant that either the United States, having won the rest of NATO to its point of view, was preparing to provide military assistance to the Czechs and Poles; or that the United States had threatened the Soviet Union with retaliation if Soviet troops crossed into Poland or Czechoslovakia. Whatever, the situation was judged critical enough to warrant moving the *Liberation* to its launch point.

Only briefly did the captain wonder whether his government knew what it was doing. He glanced at his wrist-watch. Right now, he mused, his leaders would be gathered in the underground complex at Zhihuli, about 300 miles southeast of Moscow. There, the members of the Defense Council and other important government officials would be meeting to decide the fate of the humankind. Theirs was a terrible burden to bear, but the Soviet captain could not concern himself with their problems. He had problems of his own to keep him occupied. Banishing all thought of the surface world from his mind, he gave orders for the *Liberation* to leave the *polynya* it was in and proceed out from under the ice to the open waters of the Denmark Strait some 80 miles distant.

13:00 Hours Zulu: Maneuvering for Position

The captain of the USS *Denver* grinned when the chief

Above: A submerged Typhoon-*class boomer launches its missiles. The sound of the missile tube hatch covers opening would have announced the boomer's presence and position to any U.S. hunter/killers prowling nearby. But by the time the hunter/killer could launch a torpedo, the lethal ballistic missiles would be well on their way.*

sonar operator signaled another contact. The half mile-long Thin Line Array (TLA) that had been streamed out 12 hours earlier was doing its job.

The target motion analysis program suggested that the Soviet submarine was moving on a new heading of 159 degrees. The computer had matched the noises heard by the *Denver*'s sonar to sound patterns associated with missing anechoic tiles on the submarine's hull. This sound pattern had been recorded and registered on several prior occasions when Soviet submarines had passed through convergence zones.

The captain gave orders for a course change that would angle the *Denver* ahead of the Soviet's presumed course. He then retired to his cabin to peruse the voluminous ASW-related notes he had made over the years while stalking Soviet, British, French, and even other American submarines.

Below: The red-lighted sonar room of the USS Atlanta. *Lights with a red or blue tint make it easier on the eyes when gazing at sonar and radar screens.*

18:05 Hours Zulu: On Station

The Denmark Strait is one of the most heavily mined submarine routes in the world. It was familiar territory for the Soviet captain; he had been there many times before, and had even helped to chart its mine fields. He had as yet received no reports of any recent NATO mine-laying activities, although it was possible that submarines had been used to lay new fields. He knew that the American CAPTOR mines posed the greatest threat to Soviet submarines, but he was not afraid of them, for he also knew that the titanium double-hulled construction of his *Typhoon*-class boat was virtually invulnerable to their puny 96-pound warheads.

The *Liberation* moved ahead at eight knots with the ice-sonar functioning in the passive mode. The captain paid especially close attention to the jagged peaks and blocks of ice hanging down below the surface, like an upside-down mountain chain. *Polynyas* were growing more frequent, a further sign that the Soviet boat was approaching the edge of the ice sheet some 15 miles ahead.

The captain was far more worried about American or Canadian attack submarines than he was about mines. Somewhat ominously in that regard, his sonar operators had reported hearing the rumblings of an immense ASW effort perhaps 900 miles to the south. The detonations of exploding bombs and mines, and the pinging of active radar had taken only 18 seconds to reach them from that distant battlefield. For the captain, as well as for the entire crew of *Liberation*, those sounds were a distressingly vivid reminder of what lay in store for the Soviet boat should the Americans get wind of its presence.

19:15 Hours Zulu: Confirmation

The captain of the *Denver* kneaded his face with a damp towel and took a deep breath. He was certain he had figured out the Soviet submarine commander's strategy.

Early in his career, he had served as torpedo officer on the old *Bonefish,* the last of the diesel/electric boats in the Pacific fleet. Now he recalled how the *Bonefish* had managed to sneak into the middle of a Soviet ASW exercise north of Hokkaido, Japan. While situated in what was, in effect, a ringside seat for the exercise, the *Bonefish* had used its sonar to monitor the Soviets. Of particular interest were the activities of a Soviet *Whiskey*-class attack boat, which had made a simulated attack on one of its own cruisers. The *Whiskey* boat had been able to execute its attack undetected because ASW surface ships and helicopters

had been decoyed some 50 miles away from the scene by two additional *Whiskey* boats.

It occurred to the captain that the Soviets might be employing the same decoying tactics in the present circumstances. The Soviets, he realized, were probably willing to sacrifice one or two of the *Typhoon* or *Delta IV* boats down south if by doing so they could get the *Liberation* into the optimal position from which to launch its missiles. For what was the loss of a few submarines, they might well have concluded, compared to the obliteration of the North American continent?

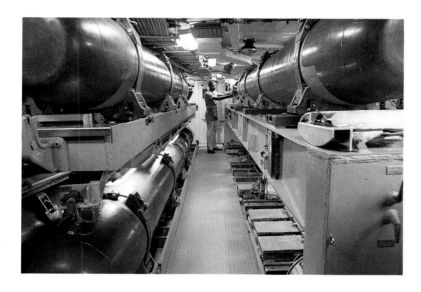

Opposite Page: A quartermaster on the USS Ray *plots the underwater position of his boat. Above Left: The torpedo room of the USS* Omaha *(SSN 692), showing Mk 48 torpedoes in their skids. Soviet* Typhoon-*class submarines like the* Liberation *are strongly built, but it is doubtful that they could withstand a salvo of Mk 48s. Above Right: Crewmen in the control room of the USS* Skipjack *(SSN 585) as the boat begins to dive. Below Left: A torpedoman on the USS* Salt Lake City *uses a meter to test electrical circuits in an Mk 48 torpedo.*

21:00 Hours Zulu: Stalemate

The Soviet captain tried not to show his impatience as the *Liberation*'s assistant captain conferred hastily with the sonar operators. Finally, after much fierce whispering, the assistant captain confirmed his commander's worst fear: an enemy attack submarine was definitely in the vicinity. Speaking in almost apologetic tone, as if this were somehow his fault, the assistant captain then added that it was a virtual certainty that the enemy boat was hunting the *Liberation.*

The captain nodded, his jaw clenched with annoyance and frustration. Of course the enemy boat was hunting the *Liberation;* of that there could be no doubt. He wondered whether the enemy boat was Canadian or American. Not that it made any difference, as the new Canadian nuclear-powered attack submarines were fully as capable as the American boats. But bearing in mind that the Canadian crews were somewhat inexperienced, he concluded that his new adversary hailed from the United States. Only a crew as experienced—and as lucky—as the Americans so often were could have found the *Liberation.*

More troubling to the Soviet captain than the fact of the American boat's presence was its proximity. The *Libera-*

tion's sonar operators had detected the American boat with a passive sonar array that had a range of only five miles. So the American boat was close, very close. And it was obviously waiting out there for some fluke of current or temperature level to give away the *Liberation*'s exact position.

At this point, there was little the Soviet captain could do about the American submarine. His own boat was already running in a silent mode, which meant that its power output had been reduced to the lowest possible levels to minimize engine noise. The coolant pumps for the nuclear reactor had been shut down, and the boat was depending on natu-

ral convection currents to circulate the liquid sodium coolant through the reactor to the heat exchanger.

Had the American submarine summoned help? Had it risen to the surface to get off a message? Only time would tell, the Soviet captain told himself. In the meantime, his boat would be quite safe from harm if it remained silent. But if it became necessary to fight, the Soviet captain was confident that his boat could kill the American boat before it killed him. He needed only the sound of a torpedo tube hatch opening, or a single ping from the enemy's active sonar to unleash *Liberation*'s wire-guided torpedoes in his enemy's direction.

Left: In the sonar room in the USS Narwhal, *blue is the color of choice. Above: The skipper on the USS* Jacksonville *peers through his periscope.*

21:20 Hours Zulu: Analysis

One of the most effective weapons in an attack submarine's arsenal is a captain who can think his way into the mind of his adversary—who can use a combination of instinct, empathy, and gut feeling to predict his enemy's next move. The American captain was just such a commander. He was certain that the Soviet captain knew the Americans were close—but he was also certain that the Soviets would not initiate offensive action until it was time for the *Liberation* to launch its missiles. Had he been in the Soviet captain's shoes (and he was, if only in his imagination), he would have conducted operations in a similar manner.

The American captain therefore had three options available to him: he could nose about until his boat banged into the Soviet boat by accident; he could use active sonar to find the Soviet boat; or he could wait until the Soviet boat opened its missile hatch covers.

The last option offered a surefire means of pinpointing the Soviet boat. Unfortunately, if the Americans waited for the sounds of opening missile hatch covers before firing a salvo of Mk 48 torpedoes, their torpedoes would not reach the Soviet boat until *after* the missiles had been launched. And even if only one SS-N-20 missile got away, that missile with its ten warheads had enough destructive power to inflict misery and death on an inconceivably vast scale.

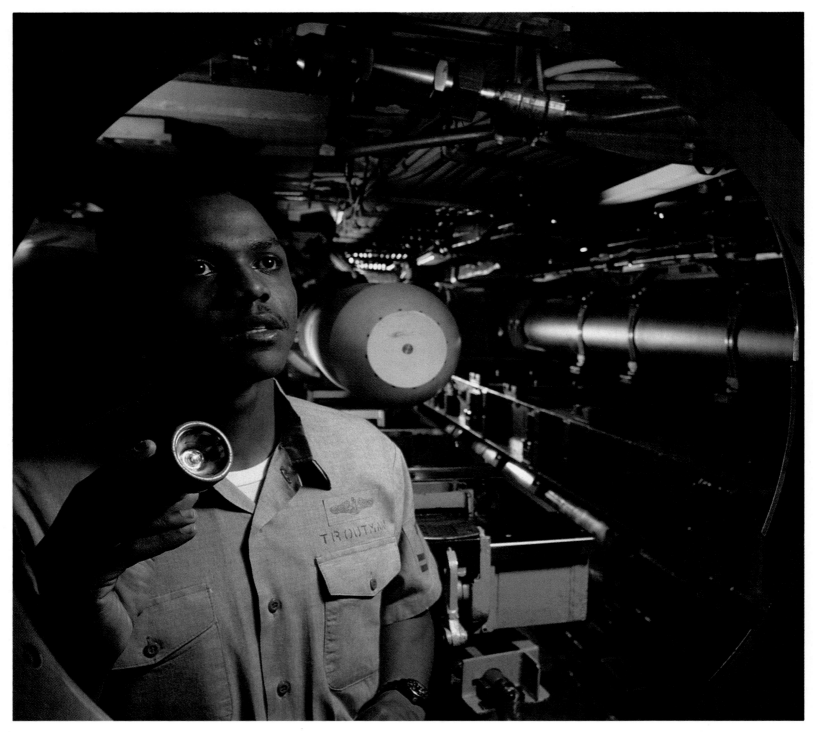

The American captain realized that he simply had to find and kill the Soviet boat before the missile hatch covers opened. But this, he knew, was easier said than done.

His brain reeled with questions. Would the Soviet commander launch his missiles at a preset time, or would he wait for permission to launch? If the latter, would the order to launch be delivered by blue-green laser, or by ELF transmission? Or would the Soviets use a communications buoy to receive a coded message sent down from a satellite? If the Soviets used a blue-green laser, it was quite possible that the captain of the *Liberation* would know only that a message had been transmitted without knowing the contents of the message. If the message was delivered by ELF, the Soviet submariners might not even pick up the transmission. But if the Soviets were employing a satellite relay, the Americans would know from the opening of the missile hatch covers that the Soviets had received their message.

After considering all this, yet another important question occurred to the American captain: the question of whether war had been declared. Having had no contact with the surface world for nearly 22 hours, he had no way of knowing. If war had been declared, he would have received at the very least a blue-green laser signal to that effect—unless the laser-transmitting satellite had been destroyed. But what if the *Denver* killed the Soviet submarine, only to find out later that war had not been declared? Would the Americans then have committed murder?

Opposite Page: A crewman on the USS Jacksonville *checks a torpedo tube. The point-of-view here is the torpedo's. Above:* Torpedo-tube inspection continues on the USS Jacksonville. *Below:* A torpedo tube on the USS Andrew Jackson, *loaded and ready to fire.*

22:55 Hours Zulu: Countermove

Twenty-five minutes had passed since the *Liberation* had released the "nixie," a torpedolike decoy with a small computer and an active sonar transmitter in place of a warhead. Once released, the current had carried the nixie away at three knots so that it was positioned well ahead of the Soviet boat. Upon reaching the end of its 6,500 foot cable, the Soviets could do nothing more than wait to see whether the Americans would take the bait, and fire a torpedo at the nixie. When that happened, the American boat would be pinpointed. In the next instant, a Soviet torpedo would be loosed at the American boat.

23:05 Hours Zulu: Confrontation

With his captain standing beside him, the *Denver's* chief sonar operator pressed the earphones tight against his ears and stared intently at the bright line on his oscilloscope. Then he tapped a button on the console. A printer whirred, and ejected a printout copy of the line. The captain inspected the printout. The computer had identified the sound as heat expansion in the Soviet submarine's liquid-metal cooling pipes, in the aft reactor compartment.

The captain struggled to maintain his composure. He wanted to be certain that the printout was evidence of the Sovi-

et submarine, not a nixie. But was it? A decoy, he knew, had to be out there somewhere. It was unthinkable that the Soviet commander would have failed to use one.

A second bright line appeared on the screen. The sonar operator tapped the glass with his pen as the line zigzagged toward the edge of the screen. The captain turned to his executive officer. He was about to give the order to stand by to fire a torpedo, but something the sonar operator did made him hesitate.

Muttering to himself, the sonar operator laid a printout of the second line over the first printout. His fingers then flashed across the keyboard. The screen cleared abruptly, then displayed an image of the two lines side-by-side. The sonar operator tapped at the keyboard, causing the two lines to merge, and looked up over his shoulder at the captain with a grimly triumphant expression.

The captain smiled faintly and nodded his head in understanding. The two lines had merged exactly; they were identical. But like human fingerprints, no two sounds are ever exactly alike—unless they come from the same recording. Which could only mean that the Soviet submarine *was* using a nixie.

*　　　*　　　*　　　*　　　*

Left: After shifting out of place, Mk 48s are re-positioned by torpedomen on the USS Ray. *Above: A torpedoman on the USS* Salt Lake City *tightens the straps that hold his Mk 48s in their skids.*

*　　　*　　　*　　　*　　　*

The *Liberation*'s chief sonar operator shook his head at his captain, who turned away in disappointment. The nixie had transmitted twice, without result. Either the Americans had not detected the nixie, or had not been fooled by it.

The captain then made his boldest move yet. First he ordered the nixie set to transmit the sound of an opening torpedo tube hatch in precisely 240 seconds; then he ordered the nixie to be cut away. The assistant captain shot him an astonished look. The decoys were worth hundreds of thousands of rubles; to lose one was bad enough, but to deliberately throw one away was practically an act of treason.

The captain ignored his assistant, as well as the implications of his deed. He would do what had to be done to accomplish his mission, and that was all there was to it. As for the charge of treason—well, he would deal with that after the fallout from World War III had settled.

The *Denver*'s chief sonar operator stiffened. He'd picked up another sound. He scribbled figures on a sheet of paper, then passed the paper to the navigator. The navigator plotted the sound's position on his chart board.

The captain saw that the first two sounds and this most recent sound were separated by approximately 350 feet. It was as if they had come from nearly opposite ends of the same boat.

A moment later, the computer identified the sound as that of an opening torpedo tube hatch cover.

The captain's stomach lurched. Had the Soviet boat found them? Was it getting ready to shoot? The captain stared at the sonar screen. There was no indication of compressed air noise. But then, the Soviets could have floated the torpedo out. The captain frowned. Something about all this did not feel right.

*　　　*　　　*　　　*　　　*

He turned to the white surface of the plot chart and stared at the penciled X-marks that indicated the Soviet boomer's position. In the submarine's dim, red light the marks were barely visible. Thinking furiously, the captain remembered that a Soviet *Typhoon*-class boat like the *Liberation* was 558 feet long. If the first two sounds came from the reactor and the third from a torpedo tube (which was located in the bow, some 350 feet from the reactor) then the distances were about right.

But still.... The captain's eyes slipped across the chart to the corner of the chart beneath it. This second chart showed current flows through the Denmark Strait. On a hunch, the captain reached for the chart and studied it intently. The chart indicated that currents in this area flowed at a speed of about 3.5 knots. The captain reminded himself that the third sound had occurred four minutes after the two sounds. Using a pocket calculator, the captain converted time and speed into distance. The number he

arrived at was 354.2—or, the distance in feet that separated the second and third sounds. From this he deduced that the *Liberation* had let a nixie float down current in order to give the Americans the false impression that their sonar had bracketed the Soviet boat.

The captain did some further calculations. To 354.2, he added the number 6,500 (the length in feet of the nixie cable). If his theory was correct, the new total (6,854.2) was the distance in feet between the third nixie signal and the *Liberation* itself. To that number he added 279, or half the length in feet of a *Typhoon*-class boat, for a total of 7,133.2—which gave him the midships point of the enemy vessel.

The captain was just about to pass the relevant coordinates to fire control when the executive officer handed him a message that the *Denver* had just received by blue-green laser transmission.

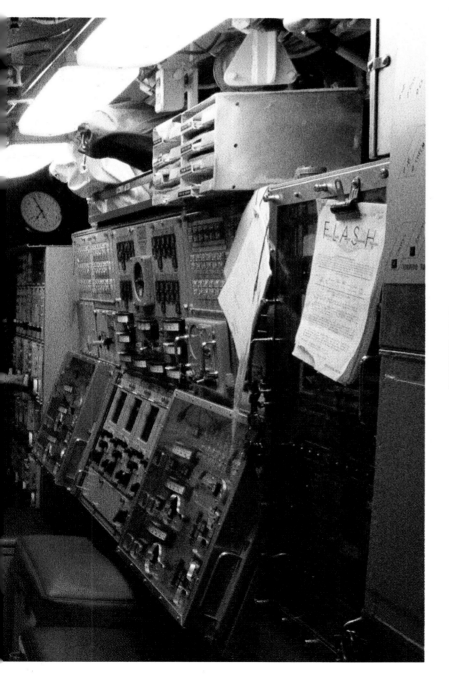

Left: Standing guard over Mk 48 torpedoes on the USS Omaha. *Above:* Soviet submariners would do well to heed the warning on this torpedo tube cover.

*　　　　*　　　　*　　　　*　　　　*

At nearly the same moment, the Soviet captain was waiting for a freshly decoded message, sent by blue-green laser, to extrude from the facsimile machine. Since the transmission had taken only 30 seconds to receive and 20 more to translate, he knew that it comprised no more than two symbols.

Around him, the members of the control room crew stood tensely at their posts. Although no one dared look away from their instruments, all were painfully aware of the captain's every move. Only the sonar operator seemed oblivious to the unfolding drama.

The captain plucked the slick, flimsy sheet from the guides. So great was his haste to read it that he tore off the bottom half as he pulled it from the machine. He turned the sheet over, wondering as he did whether it would fall to him to start World War III. From the corner of his eye, he saw the missile control officer flip up the red covers over the missile arming switches.

The single symbol on the sheet stunned him. For an instant, his mind could not absorb its import.

The symbol indicated that the *Liberation* was to stand down and return to base!

The Soviet captain clutched a handhold to steady himself, then closed his eyes and uttered a short prayer of thanksgiving before he shared the news with his crew.

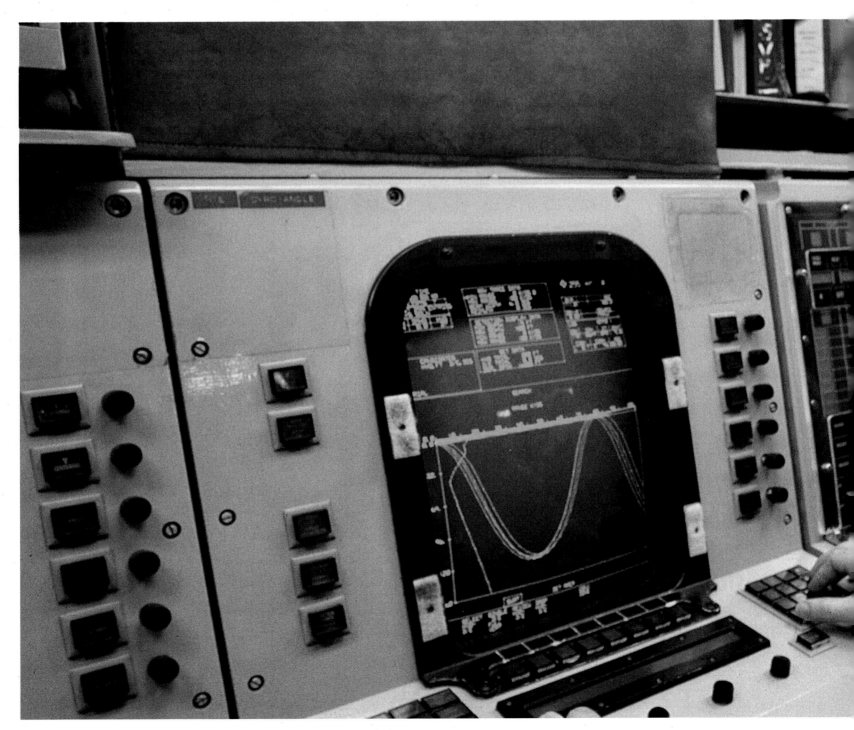

*   *   *   *   *

Aboard the USS *Denver,* the same scene was being repeated as the captain read a similar message to the control room crew. Somehow, the captain thought, the politicians had found a way to defuse the crisis. Maybe the Soviet conservatives had been ousted from power; maybe the United States and its allies had capitulated to Soviet demands to reestablish their rule in Eastern Europe. Or maybe, just maybe, both sides had decided that the whole thing was just not worth a nuclear war. Whatever the reason, the captain was profoundly relieved at the outcome.

Yet although the war was over before it had even begun, beneath the waters of the Denmark Strait there remained some unfinished business to take care of. Both the American and Soviet captains now faced the same problem: how to let each other know that they had no hostile intentions,

so that a move to withdraw would not invite a torpedo.

Theirs was a dilemma that epitomized the entire Cold War experience. And like the Cold War, it was a dilemma without any readily apparent solution.

Left: A look at the torpedo fire control panel on the USS Salt Lake City. *Above: Launching torpedoes on the USS* Salt Lake City.

Active sonar.
Sonar that transmits a sound wave, which is intercepted by the sender when its echo bounces off a solid object.

Anechoic tile.
Sound-deadening or absorbing tiles of rubbery material placed on submarine hulls.

Antisubmarine warfare (ASW).
Series of techniques and weapons systems used to detect and destroy enemy submarines.

Attack submarine (SS).
A type of submarine whose main purpose is to find and destroy enemy submarines.

Background noise.
Natural noises in the sea emanating from animals, fish, and earth and ice movements.

Ballistic missile.
A rocket-powered missile that maintains its course and trajectory on the initial impulse of its engines, with only minor corrections from a guidance system.

Blue-green laser.
A type of laser used in surface-to-subsurface communications. Water is relatively impervious to coherent light beams, which tend to be reflected and scattered by floating particles. Blue-green light penetrates water with relative ease. The coherent beam of light generated by a laser in the blue-green portion of the spectrum can penetrate sea water to two hundred feet or more.

Boomer.
Nickname for a ballistic missile-carrying submarine.

Bow-mounted sonar.
Sonar transmitter and receiver system mounted on the bow of a submarine or surface ship to "look" forward.

CAPTOR Mine.
Encapsulated Torpedo. An antisubmarine mine containing an Mk 46 Mod 4 torpedo that is activated acoustically by a passing submarine.

Chain reaction.
The process of nuclear fission whereby a neutron strikes the nucleus of another atom and splits it, knocking additional neutrons free to split other atoms.

Choke Points.
Areas where landmasses and/or the sea bed interact to form narrow and shallow corridors through which transiting submarines must pass. Examples of choke points include the Bering Strait between Alaska and the Soviet Union, the Denmark Strait between Greenland and Iceland, and the Norwegian Sea.

Circular Error of Probability (CEP).
The radius of an imaginary circle that is centered on a point into which 50 percent of all warheads of a given missile type can be expected to fall. A measure of a missile's accuracy.

Cluster Guard.
NATO code name for the anechoic tile system used on Soviet submarines.

Communications buoy.
A floating radio transmitter released by ships or submarines.

Continental shelf.
The underwater portion of a continental plate.

Convection currents.
Movement of a liquid caused by temperature differentials across its volume.

Conventional power.
The form of power generated by diesel/electric engines.

Convergence zone.
An underwater area where arcing sound waves meet and cancel out one another.

Cruise missile.
A guided missile that has terrain-following radar and flies at slower speeds and lower altitudes than ballistic missiles. May have nuclear or conventional warheads.

Cruise missile launching submarine (SSGN).
Submarine equipped to carry and launch cruise missiles.

Decapitating strike.
A nuclear missile strike aimed at enemy command control centers and at strategic weapons. The objective of such a strike is to destroy the enemy's ability to retaliate.

Deep Scatter Layer (DSL).
A zone in the ocean composed of thick and thin layers of microscopic animal and plant life, that reflects and scatters sound waves.

Denmark Strait.
The North Atlantic sea passage between Iceland and Greenland.

Diesel/electric motor.
The motor used in non-nuclear, or conventionally powered, submarines. Air-breathing diesel engines provide propulsion on the surface; electric motors powered by batteries are used when submerged.

Double hulling.
The construction technique whereby a submarine's main hull is protected by an outer shell. A common practice in Soviet submarines.

Electron.
A negatively charged subatomic particle in the nucleus of an atom.

Extremely Low Frequency (ELF).
Long-wave radio waves capable of penetrating water to depths of up to 350 feet.

First strike.
A surprise attack with nuclear weapons.

GIUK Barrier.
Greenland, Iceland, United Kingdom. Antisubmarine network of patrolling submarines, sonar listening devices, magnetic anomaly detectors, and hydrophones. Would be supplemented in wartime with surface patrols.

Heat exchanger.
A tank in which a liquid used to cool a heat source heats another, cold liquid, thus transferring, or exchanging, its heat.

Hunter/killer.
Nickname for an attack submarine.

Hydrophone.
Underwater listening device.

Ice sonar.
Sonar system designed to detect the underwater contours of an ice sheet.

Intercontinental ballistic missile (ICBM).
A land-based ballistic missile with a range of 2,500 miles or more.

InterGerman Border (IGB).
The border between East and West Germany.

Kiloton.
Nuclear explosive force measurement. One kiloton is equal in force to 1,000 tons of TNT.

Liquid metal-cooled reactor.
A nuclear reactor in which a liquid metal like sodium or lead-bismuth is used as a cooling medium.

Magnetic Anomaly Detector (MAD).
An instrument that detects changes in the Earth's magnetic field caused by the presence of a large body of metal.

Maneuvering Reentry Vehicles (MaEV).
Nuclear missile warheads capable of changing course after reentry to strike a target.

Marginal Sea Ice Zone (MIZ).
The edge of the Arctic or Antarctic Ocean ice sheets.

Mines.
Explosive devices placed in the ocean. They detonate when their sensors are disturbed by a passing ship or submarine.

Mk 48 torpedo.
The standard torpedo in service in U.S. submarines.

Modification (MOD).
Any major change to an American weapons system, i.e. Mk 1, Mod 4 = model number 1, change four.

Multiple Independent Reentry Vehicle (MIRV).
A device mounted in the nose of a ballistic missile that carries a single nuclear warhead. A "MIRVed" missile carries several of these devices in its nose. The "bus" in which the MIRVs are grouped is a rocket-powered container that separates from the missile during the terminal stage of the missile's flight. The bus then releases the MIRVs, which proceed to their preassigned targets.

Mutual Assured Destruction (MAD).
The unofficial, but practical theory of nuclear warfare whereby both sides are held in check by the threat of overwhelming mutual destruction.

National Command Authority.
The president or his constitutional successors. The latter could be the Vice-President, the Speaker of the House of Representatives, the President Pro-tempore of the Senate, and so on.

National Emergency Airborne Command Post.
An aircraft fitted with extensive communications equipment that allows the president or his military appointee to direct U.S. response in a nuclear war.

National Military Command Authority Center.
The Armed Forces chain of command.

Neutron.
An uncharged subatomic particle in the nucleus of an atom.

Nixie.
Nickname for a decoy that simulates the sounds of a submarine or its weapons.

North Atlantic Treaty Organization (NATO).
The military alliance between the U.S., Canada, Turkey, and most of the nations of Western Europe (France being the most notable exception). Established in April 1949 to provide a counterweight to the Soviet military presence in Eastern Europe.

Optical Submarine Communications Aerospace Relay (OSCAR).
A communications system that involves a geostationary satellite and a blue-green laser, and that allows one-way communication with U.S. submarines.

Passive sonar.
Sonar that detects sound waves traveling through the water, much like a microphone picks up sounds in the air.

PBXN-103.
Type of explosive used in the Mk 48 torpedo.

PLARBS.
Soviet acronym for strategic ballistic missile submarine (boomer).

Polynya.
An area within the Arctic ice sheet that is relatively ice free. Submarines operating under the Arctic ice use such areas to surface.

Pressurized water-cooled reactor.
Nuclear reactor using water under pressure as a cooling mechanism.

Proton.
A positively charged subatomic particle in the nucleus of an atom.

Purpose-built.
The term used to describe any submarine or surface vessel designed from the keel up for a specific purpose.

Salinity level.
The degree, or concentration, of salt in sea water.

Sea lines of communication (SLOC).
Shipping routes.

Snorkel.
German invention of WWII. A tube extended to the surface that allows a non-nuclear submarine to operate its diesel engines while traveling submerged.

Sonar.
The transmission of an electronic signal underwater by means of an oscillator operating at a fixed frequency. When the signal strikes an object, it is reflected. A receiver coupled to a computer measures the length of time between transmission and reception and calculates range and bearing.

Sonar array.
An assembly of transmitters or receivers. Arrays increase precision.

Sound Surveillance System (SOSUS).
A system of passive sonar detectors and hydrophones, usually emplaced on the ocean floor, that are designed to listen for and track submarines in specific areas.

SS.
Conventionally powered (diesel/electric) attack submarine.

SSBN.
Strategic ballistic missile-carrying submarine (boomer).

SSN.
Nuclear-powered attack submarine.

Strata.
Layers of sea water of differing temperatures, salinity, and so on.

Strategic Arms Limitation Treaty (SALT).
Series of negotiations conducted between the United States and the Soviet Union aimed at reducing the number of nuclear weapons in both arsenals.

Submarine launched ballistic missile (SLBM).
A ballistic missile specially designed and built for underwater launching from a submarine.

Surge.
The process by which a fleet of submarines is moved to warfighting stations in advance of a declaration of war. May also be applied to aircraft and other vehicles.

Take Charge and Move Out (TACAMO).
An airborne system developed by the U.S. Navy for the command and control of a submarine fleet in wartime.

Target Motion Analysis (TMA).
A computerized system for determining the bearing and measuring the range to an underwater target.

Thermocline.
A layer of ocean water in which the temperature declines at a relatively rapid rate.

Thin Line Array (TLA).
A passive sonar detection system mounted on a very long cable and trailed behind a submarine.

Towed array passive receiver.
An array of passive sonar receivers mounted on a sled and trailed behind a submarine at the end of a harness. Such an array is outside the turbulence of the submarine and is very sensitive.

Transparency.
Refers to ability of a sonar signal to penetrate water.

Vertical Launch System.
A launching system developed for surface ships and submarines whereby missiles are launched from vertical holders.

Zulu.
Internationally accepted code word for the time at Greenwich, England. Greenwich time is used as a reference standard when operating across time zones.